AF265894

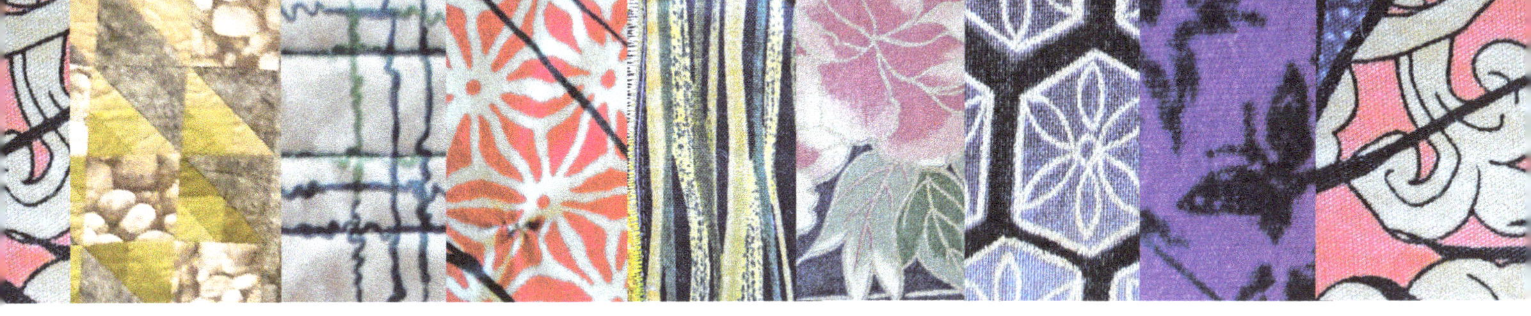

THE FABRIC
OF MEMORY

Textile art inspired by the history of the World War II incarceration of Japanese Americans at Heart Mountain

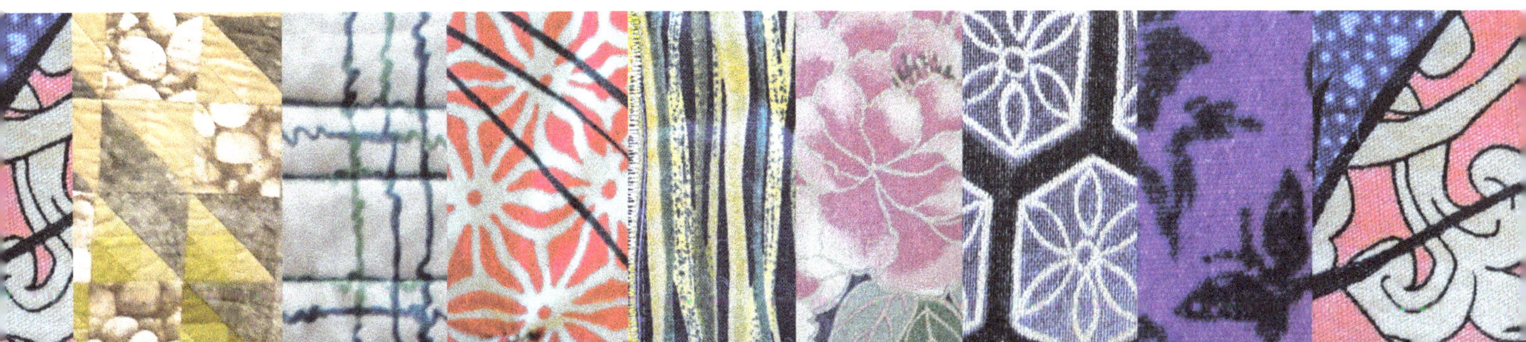

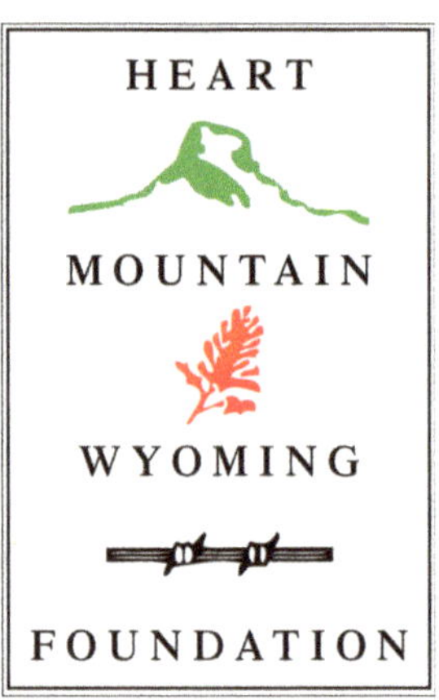

Second Printing: 2018
ISBN 9780997863208
Heart Mountain Wyoming Foundation
1539 Road 19
Powell, Wyoming 82435
www.heartmountain.org

Photography: Kathy Lichtendahl and Northwest College Photo Theme Seminar
Book Design: Claire Cella
Production: Jeanne Knudsen, Brian Liesinger and Danielle Constein

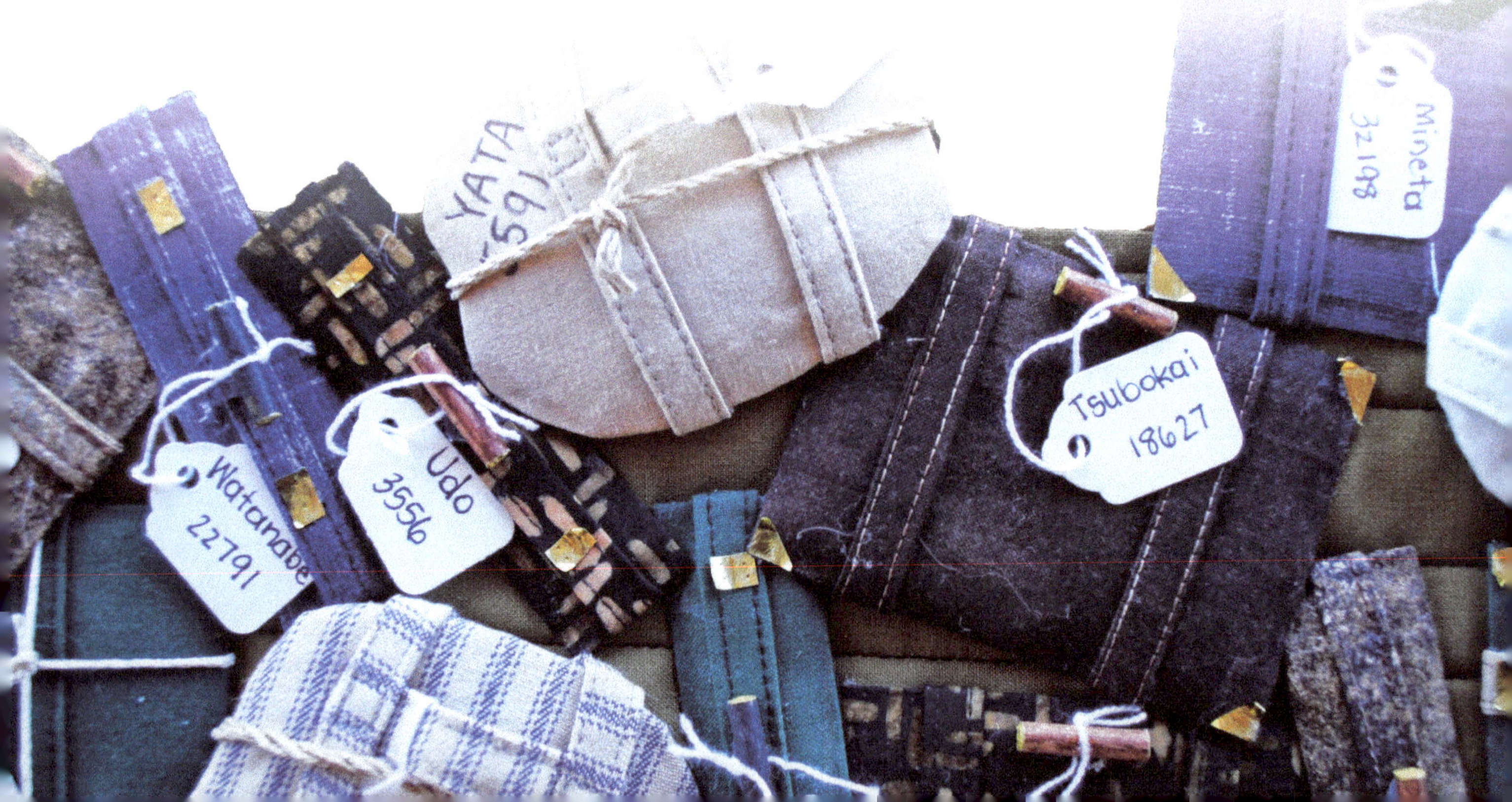

DEDICATION

The Textile Artists of the Greater Yellowstone would like to dedicate this book to Japanese Americans who were incarcerated at Heart Mountain from 1942–1945.

ACKNOWLEDGEMENTS

Exhibit Curator

Jeanne Knudsen

Assistant Curator

Jan Wilbur

Heart Mountain Interpretive Center Staff

Brian Liesinger

Danielle Constein

Dakota Russell

Kate Wilson

Sharyl McDowell

Anna Clifton

Photography

Instructor: Kathy Lichtendahl

Northwest College Photo Theme Seminar Students: Erin Buhler, Ismael Dominguez, Jordan Eidem, Justine Hoser, Colby Jones, Kara Mullins, Casey Oleson, Victoria Olson, Travis Russell

Early in 2016, I met a number of women from a collective called the Textile Artists of the Greater Yellowstone (TAGY). They were doing a project on Heart Mountain and had paid the Heart Mountain Interpretive Center a visit in search of inspiration. After their visit, they went off to conduct research, apply their individual lenses to history, and design a series of textile art pieces based on their experiences. They casually called themselves "quilters." But when they revealed their works, we discovered that these women were far too modest for the level of skill and artistry they applied to their pieces.

It was through the initiative and generosity of TAGY that we were able to open a unique exhibit featuring their pieces in our Ford Foundation gallery in 2016 titled *The Fabric of Memory*. It was the first of its kind at the Heart Mountain Interpretive Center. As a centerpiece to the exhibit, we featured a quilt by former Heart Mountain incarceree Naoko Yoshimura Ito. When her piece, titled "Letting Go," was donated in 2015, we were ecstatic about exhibiting it. With the TAGY works as companions to Ito's larger quilt, the resulting exhibit elicited such an enthusiastic response from the public that we had to extend the exhibit's run—twice. Moved by the response from visitors near and far, TAGY generously donated their pieces to the Heart Mountain Wyoming Foundation—in addition to donating funding for this book, which features all of the pieces in the exhibit. I am grateful and proud to have these works of art as part of our collection, and we hope to give the exhibit extended reach, both through this book and by turning it into a traveling exhibition.

These artists set out to illustrate, with textiles, what the unjust incarceration of Japanese Americans at Heart Mountain during World War II meant to them. In doing so, they joined us in owning and interpreting this often-overlooked chapter of American history. They allowed us to extend our mission goals to educate the public about the past and remind them about the importance of standing up for social justice today. Collectively, they represent a profound contemporary reaction to history, and they have greatly enriched this National Historic Landmark site with their art.

– BRIAN LIESINGER, EXECUTIVE DIRECTOR
HEART MOUNTAIN WYOMING FOUNDATION

THE **INTERPRETIVE CENTER**

In August 2011, the Heart Mountain Wyoming Foundation opened the Heart Mountain Interpretive Center, a world-class museum dedicated to educating the public about the World War II Japanese American incarceration experience.

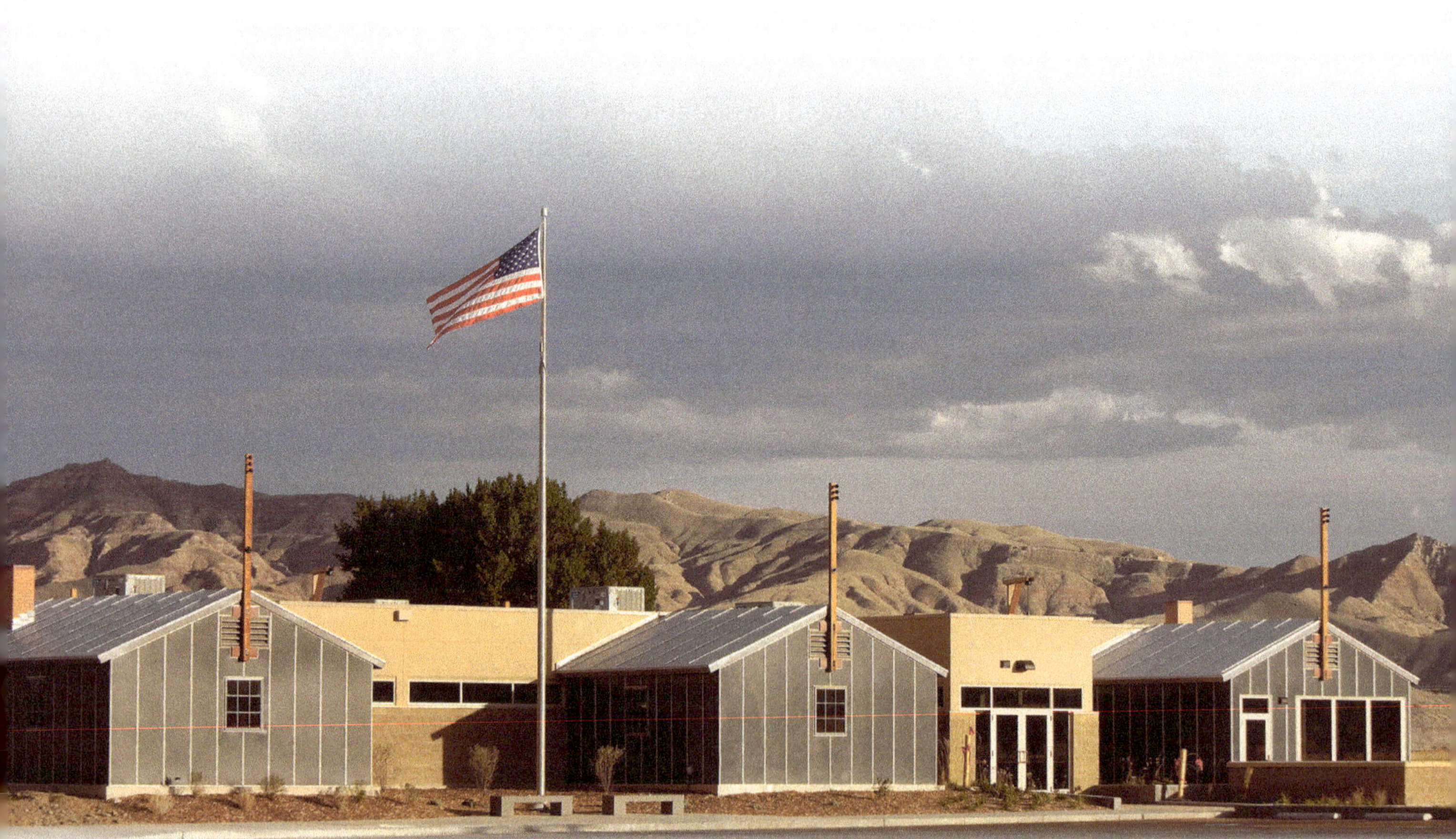

A NATIONAL HISTORIC LANDMARK

In the wake of the December 7, 1941 attack on Pearl Harbor by the Japanese Imperial Army nearly 120,000 Japanese Americans were singled out, swept up, and unjustly incarcerated in isolated camps across the country. One of those confinement camps was built in the shadow of Heart Mountain in Northwest Wyoming. The original "Heart Mountain Relocation Center" opened in August of 1942 and confined more than 14,000 people during its three-year existence.

Through photographs, artifacts, oral histories, and interactive exhibits guests to the Heart Mountain Interpretive Center experience life at Heart Mountain through the eyes of Japanese and Japanese Americans who were confined there during World War II. The Center provides an overview of the wartime incarceration, including a history of anti-Asian prejudice and the factors leading to confinement. The exhibits focus on the incarceration experience, the diverse personal responses to imprisonment, related constitutional issues and violations of civil liberties, and the broader issues of race and social justice in America.

In addition to the award-winning Interpretive Center, there are original historic buildings and other features at this National Historic Landmark site. A replicated Honor Roll Memorial commemorates those from Heart Mountain who went on to serve in World War II. The memorial is part of an interpretive walking tour. Also on the site are a reconstructed guard tower, a victory garden, a root cellar, and an original barrack that was successfully saved from demolition and returned to the site in 2015.

With the opening of the Center in 2011 and the site's significant progress since, the Heart Mountain Wyoming Foundation looks to the future and continues its efforts to remind the nation about the importance of tolerance and the need to balance a concern for national security with a commitment to protect the individual civil rights of all citizens. The site continues to evolve, with future interpretation and preservation projects in the works. This includes pursuing special projects and exhibits like *The Fabric of Memory*. Through artistic mediums, the work of artists, and the engagement of the community, the Foundation hopes to further strengthen a connection to this historic place and our shared history to build a better, more just future.

The Textile Artists of the Greater Yellowstone, often referred to as TAGY, began in 2007. After driving to Billings, Montana, once a month for many years to attend a fiber art group called the "Women of Artistic Vision," Kathy Lichtendahl and I decided to see if there was an interest in starting a group for fiber artists in the Big Horn Basin of Wyoming. The first TAGY meeting was in April of 2007 with 10–12 people in attendance, and the group has now grown to over 20 members who regularly attend the monthly meetings.

Each year we choose to challenge ourselves to make a themed quilt exhibit. For many years our challenges had been similar to those of other fiber art groups. Our challenge for 2016, however, was the "Heart Mountain Relocation Center" because of the history it brings to the communities we live in and come from. In early August 2015, the TAGY group visited the Interpretive Center together, and some of the members returned five or six times for further inspiration and to ensure the accuracy of their notes before they began to create their pieces.

Through tears and laughter, 17 TAGY artists created 22 original pieces of art depicting how the "Heart Mountain Relocation Center" made us feel. We did not anticipate the huge welcoming response the art quilts would receive from not only the staff at Heart Mountain, but also the visiting public.

The Textile Artists of the Greater Yellowstone hope that our permanent donation of this exhibit to the Heart Mountain Wyoming Foundation will not only be viewed by thousands but will help educate future generations about this part of American history
so that it may never be repeated.

**- JEANNE M. KNUDSEN
TEXTILE ARTISTS OF THE GREATER YELLOWSTONE**

A quilt is a textile with layers woven together using a distinct technique.

This book represents an exhibit of 22 fabric artworks that were displayed at the Heart Mountain Interpretive Center in 2016. They were made by 17 women of the Textile Artists of the Greater Yellowstone (TAGY), who hail from the Wyoming towns of Cody, Powell, Meeteetse, Lovell, Sheridan, and Thermopolis which are localities near the Interpretive Center.

Also displayed with these works was a quilt by Naoko Yoshimura Ito, a Japanese American who, as a child, was forcibly removed from her home in 1942 and incarcerated at the "Heart Mountain Relocation Center" for three years with her family.

The artists featured in this book employed their talents to express experiences and to make meaning of memory. The pieces they created feature a great variety in material and method. Ito's quilt is a meditation on her past—a way to make peace with years of hardship, injustice, and loss. The TAGY textiles were made by sewing patches of fabric while drawing from personal reactions to the Interpretive Center exhibits and the stories they reveal.

The TAGY artists discovered ways to stitch together the Japanese American experience and their own lives. The collection presents viewers with traditional techniques of fabric arts in addition to creative processes borrowed from other arts, including collage, origami, dyeing, beading, appliqué, silk screening, and spray painting. The women of TAGY also experimented, incorporating vintage silk kimonos, Shibori dyed fabrics, documents, and even real barbed wire.

We invite you to explore the many layers within "The Fabric of Memory," and the various threads that tie us all to the spirit and stories of the Japanese American experience.

NAOKO YOSHIMURA ITO

"Letting Go," the large story quilt central to *The Fabric of Memory*, was made in 1990 by Naoko Yoshimura Ito. Ito was raised in San Francisco's Japantown, where her father ran the Hokubei Hotel. In 1942, her family—along with 120,000 other Japanese Americans living on the West Coast of the United States—was forcibly removed from their home and ordered to report to War Relocation Authority Centers. Her family, one of the last to leave the city, was sent to the "Heart Mountain Relocation Center" between Cody and Powell, Wyoming.

As a teenager living at Heart Mountain, Naoko attended school and graduated from the Heart Mountain High School. When the camp closed, Naoko and her family returned to San Francisco to resume operating the hotel, lucky that their personal property had not been vandalized or stolen. A few years later, Naoko married Takeshi "Peter" Ito and the couple went on to raise three children in Berkeley, California. During this period of her life, she worked as a secretary for the Berkeley Unified School District and developed an avid interest in and talent for quilting.

Naoko was one of the founding members and a former president of the East Bay Heritage Quilters. In 1983, she was instrumental in organizing the first United States/Japan Quilt Symposium in Tokyo and Kyoto, and continued to coordinate the cross-cultural event for four years. For more than 17 years, she has taught quilting at the Japanese Cultural and Community Center of Northern California. Her own quilt work has been exhibited in quilt shows and featured in books such as *Making Home from War*, *Story Quilts: Telling your Tale in Fabric* and *From Our Side of the Fence*. Her most well-known is "Letting Go"—a visual memory Naoko remembered from life at Heart Mountain. In 1996, the Southern Poverty Law Center featured an image of the quilt as a part of their Teaching Tolerance project. The project was an extension of the nonprofit's legal and educational efforts in response to an alarming increase in hate crime among youth. The poster helped teach tolerance, respect and community building to students.

In August 2015, Naoko came to Wyoming for the annual Heart Mountain Pilgrimage and presented the quilt in person to the Heart Mountain Wyoming Foundation, entrusting the Interpretive Center staff with its care.

"Letting Go"

During World War II, because of my Japanese ancestry, we were incarcerated in the Relocation Camp in Heart Mountain, Wyoming. We could only take what we could carry, which meant no pets.

One day in camp, my brother and I found a small bird and captured it and had Father make a cage for it. We noticed that the mother bird, fighting her fear of humans, brought her baby bird a worm each day for one week. Since we could no longer stand separating the mother and baby, we let our pet go. I was fifteen years old.

Naoko Yoshimura Ito
Berkeley, California

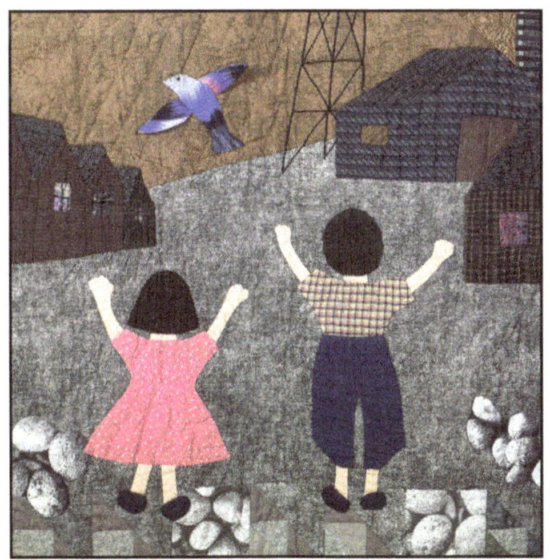

Naoko Yoshimura Ito's "Letting Go."

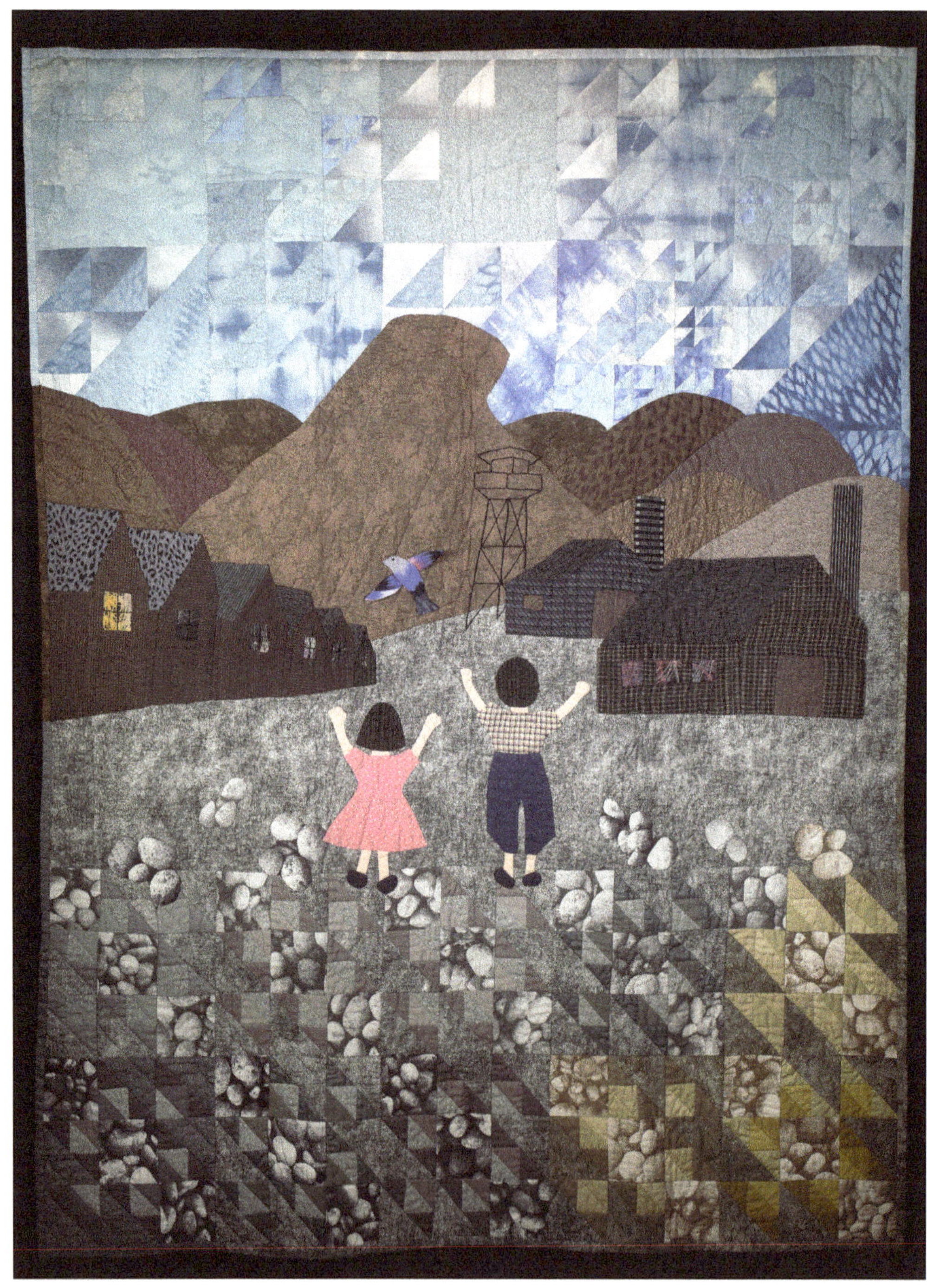

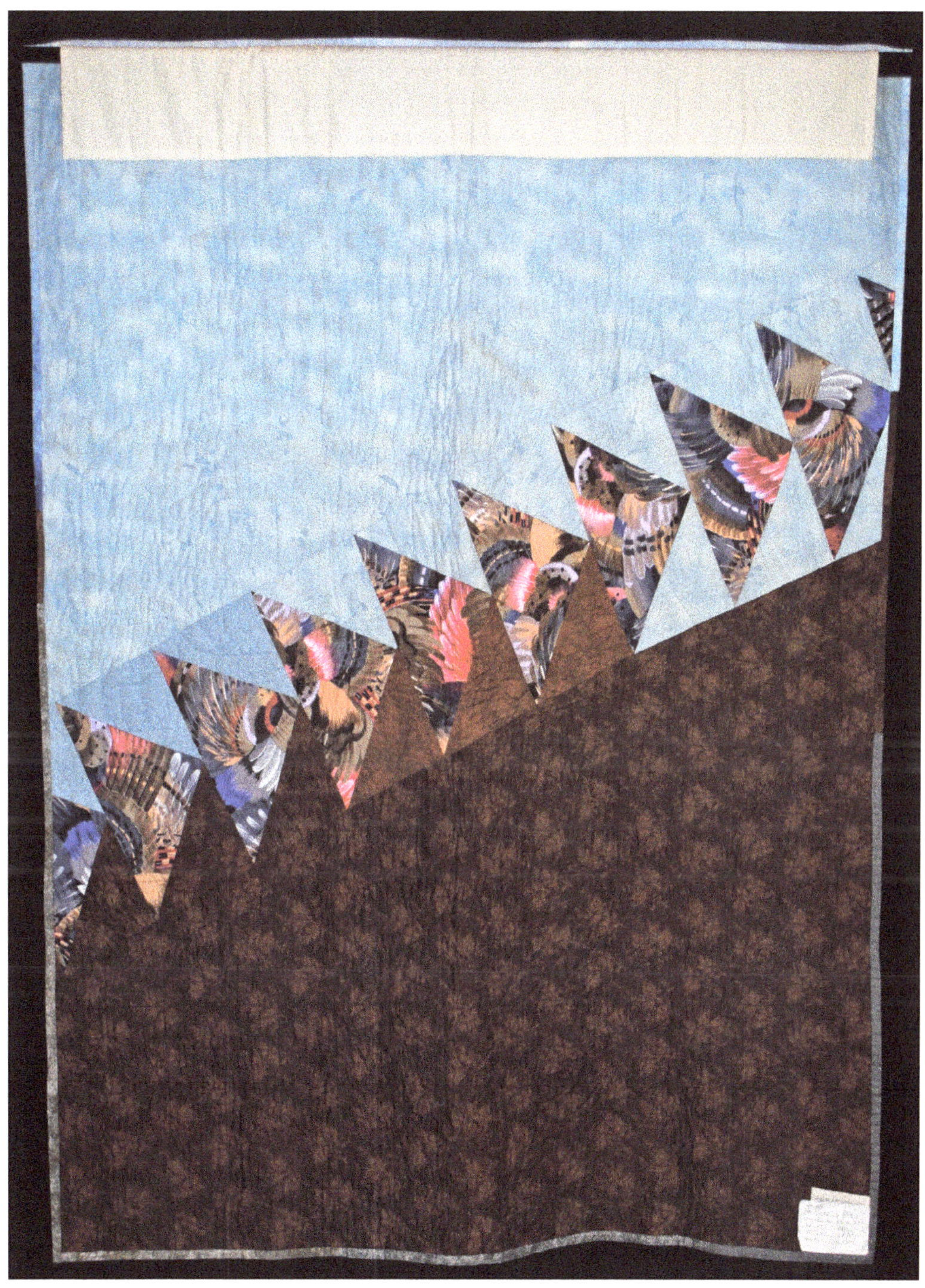

Naoko Yoshimura Ito's "Letting Go" (back).

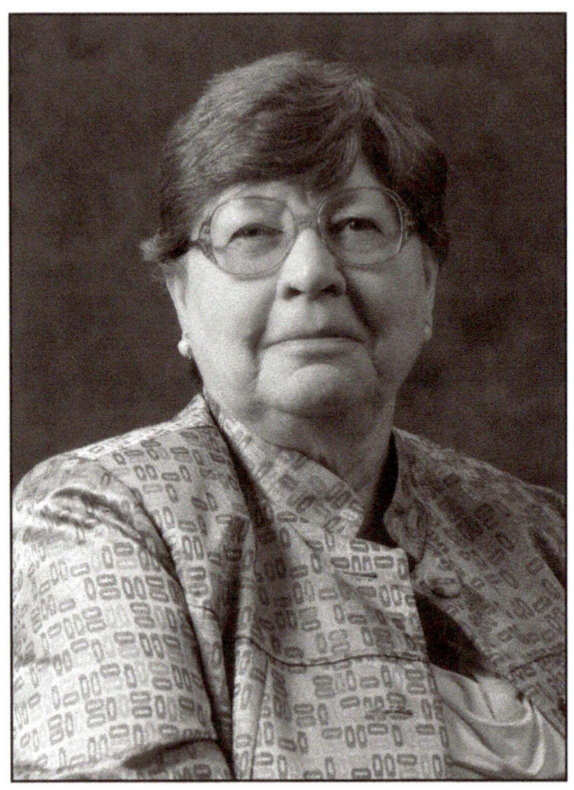

Karling Abernathy
Cody, Wyoming

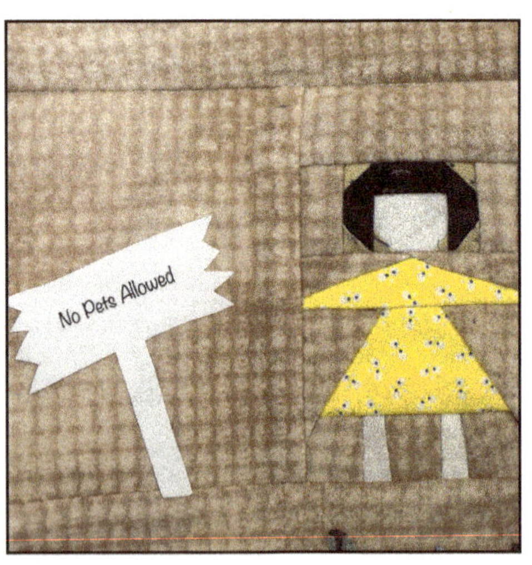

"PLUCKED AND PLACED"

I discussed with a friend the implications of being removed from one's home with few belongings and placed in a foreign environment. Like dolls in a dollhouse, people were "plucked and placed" with no choice in the matter.

Born after World War II, as a native Wyomingite, I do not recall that we learned about the "Relocation Center" in either fourth grade or eighth grade history.

I have gained more knowledge since moving to Cody in 1990. No due process; no pets; bring only what you can carry. All of these concepts were new to my understanding of what living in an internment camp entailed. The more I learn about how American citizens were treated, the more concern I have that this might happen again. It should not.

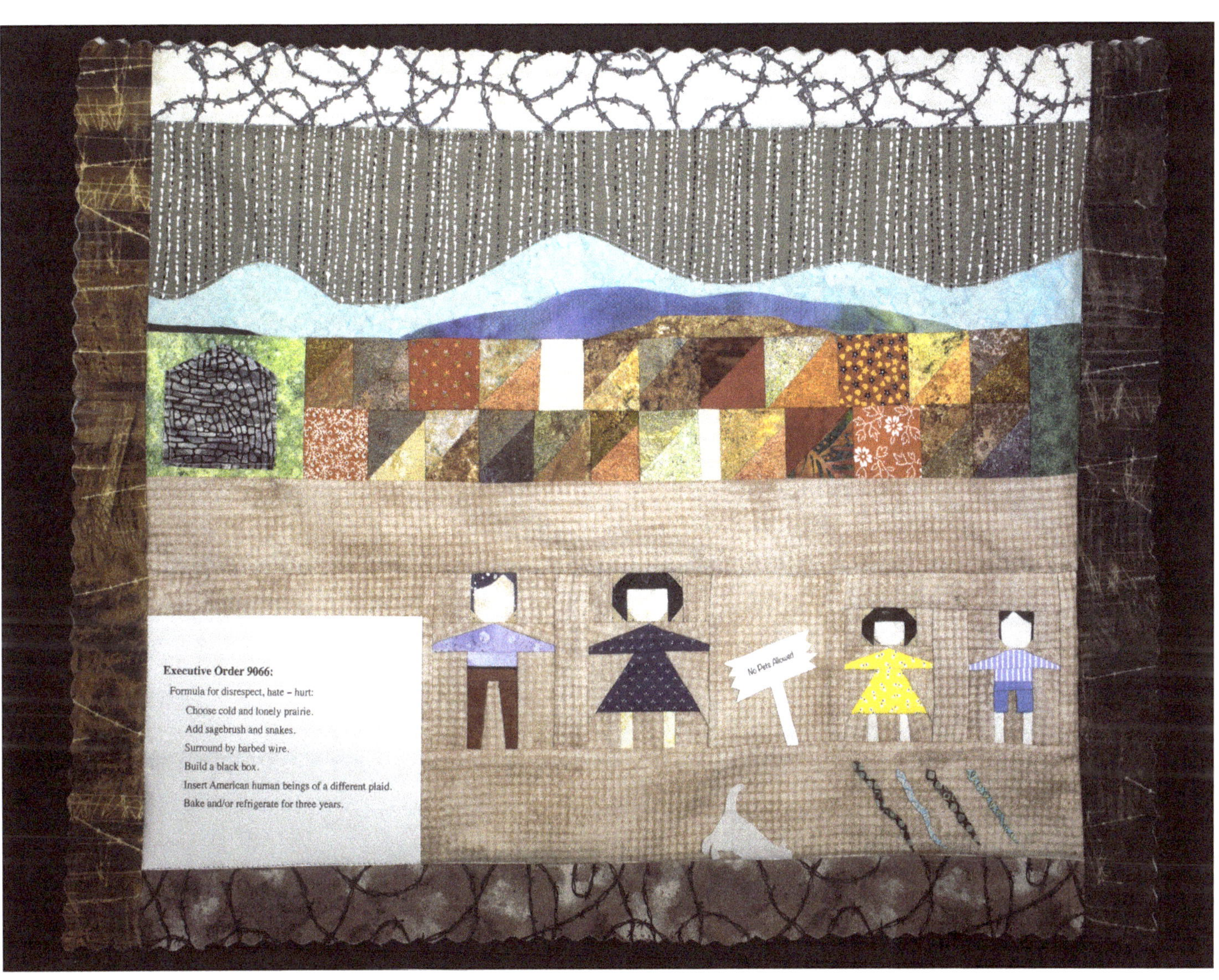

Executive Order 9066:
Formula for disrespect, hate – hurt:
Choose cold and lonely prairie.
Add sagebrush and snakes.
Surround by barbed wire.
Build a black box.
Insert American human beings of a different plaid.
Bake and/or refrigerate for three years.
No Pets Allowed!

"Peaceful Internees"

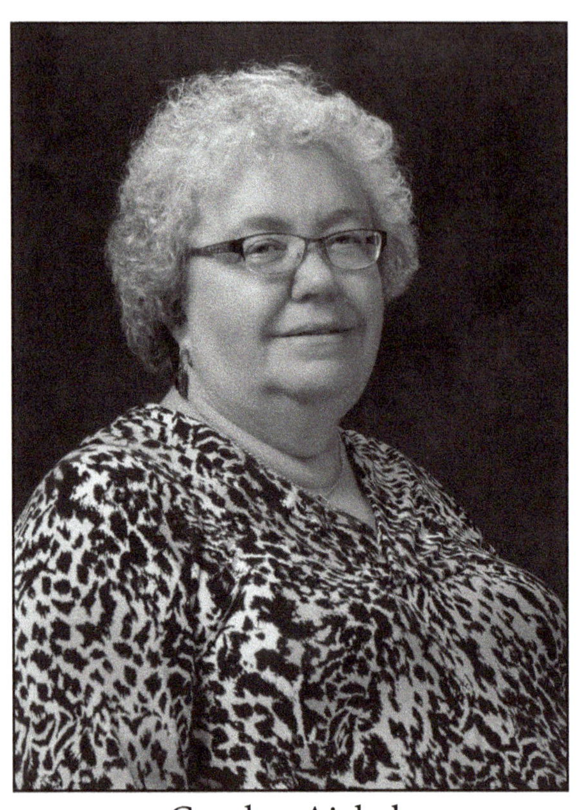

Carolyn Aichele
Lovell, Wyoming

Trapped in old Wyoming barbed wire are fabric cranes representing the Americans of Japanese descent illegally imprisoned at Heart Mountain Internment Center.

One of the reasons this project resonates with me is my personal experience with unfair childhood incarceration. As an 8-year-old foster child, I was incarcerated behind barbed wire at a juvenile detention facility in Oregon.

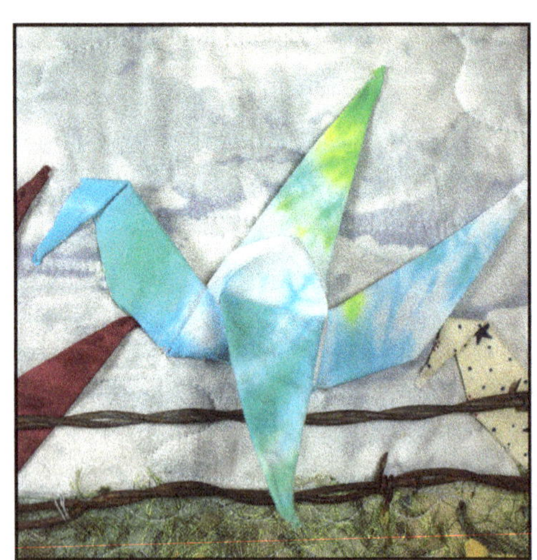

Visitor Comments:

"These quilts have caught the essence of the tragic circumstances of the miscarriage of justice."

–Anonymous

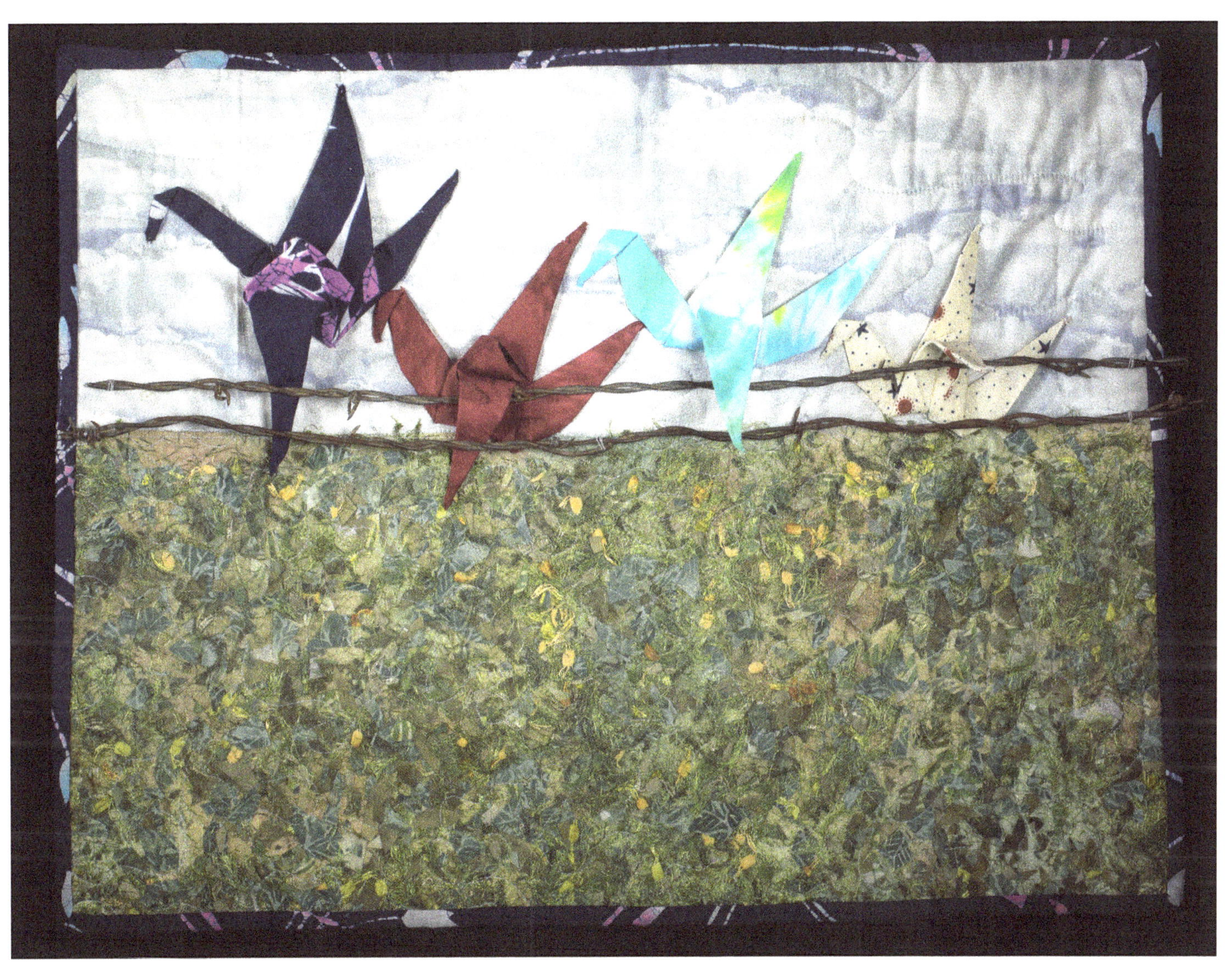

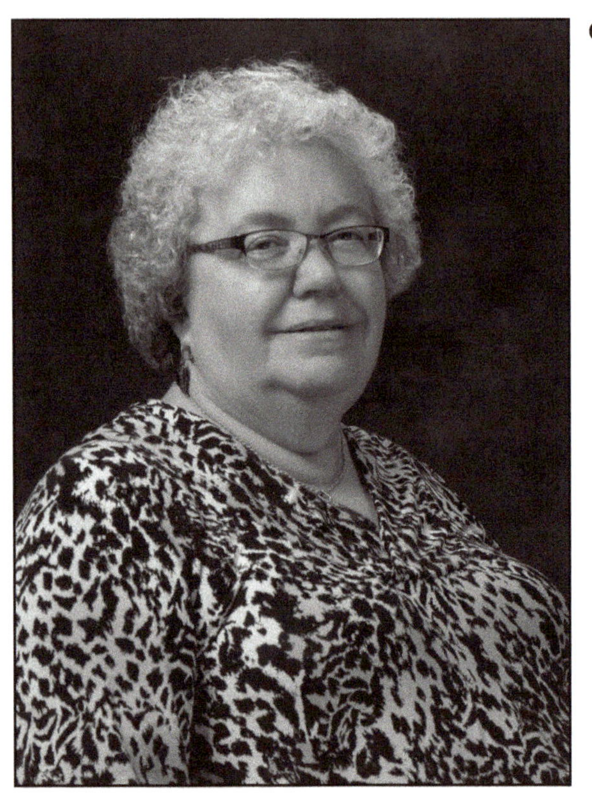

Carolyn Aichele
Lovell, Wyoming

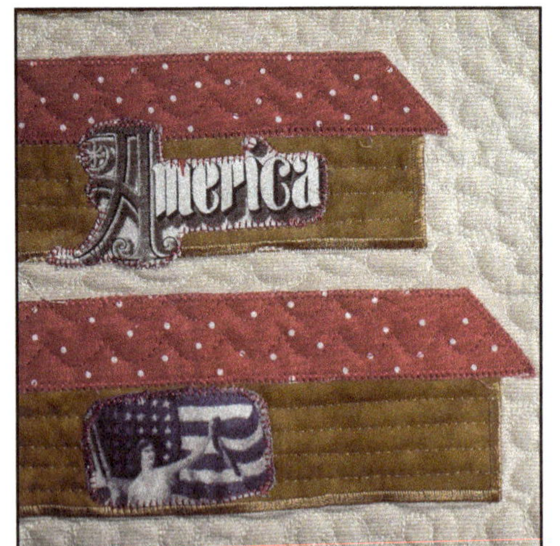

"Heart Mountain Kimono"

Vintage Japanese kimono fabrics were used to represent Heart Mountain with prisoner barracks in the foreground.

I purchased the vintage kimono fabrics at the Quilt Museum in Lincoln, Nebraska.

Visitor Comments:

"An important way for local artists to engage seriously, creatively, critically with the fabric of our cultural landscape."
–Mary, from Wyoming

"Love the various 'take-aways' the quilters experienced."

–Anonymous

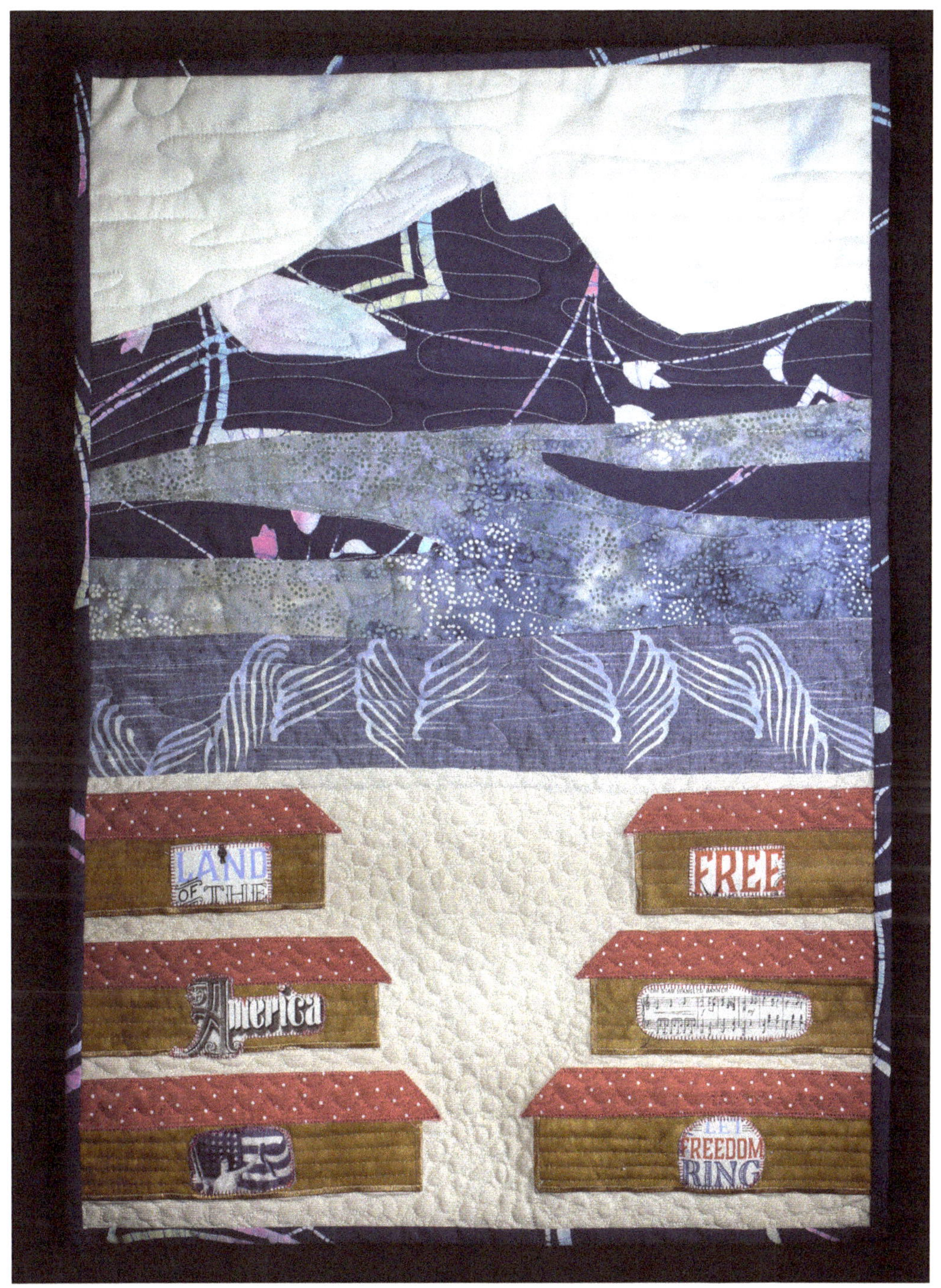

LAND OF THE
FREE
America
LET FREEDOM RING

"Not By Choice"

Ginger Dager
Cody, Wyoming

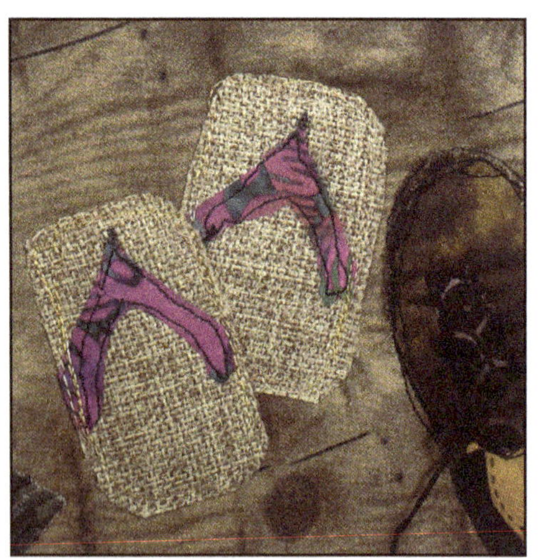

These Kanji symbols represent a tale of a people forced from their homes. These Americans found:

Beauty in the shadow of Heart Mountain.

Honor in the American flag they loved.

Strength in their families.

Hope in the vegetables that they were able to grow in the land where they had never grown before: *mizuna, daikon,* and *takana.*

Freedom came eventually and the last possessions they gathered were their shoes, always left by the door in the Japanese tradition.

This quilt, in 5 symbols, conveys some of the emotion these families must have felt when they were taken from their homes, not by choice, to a place called Heart Mountain.

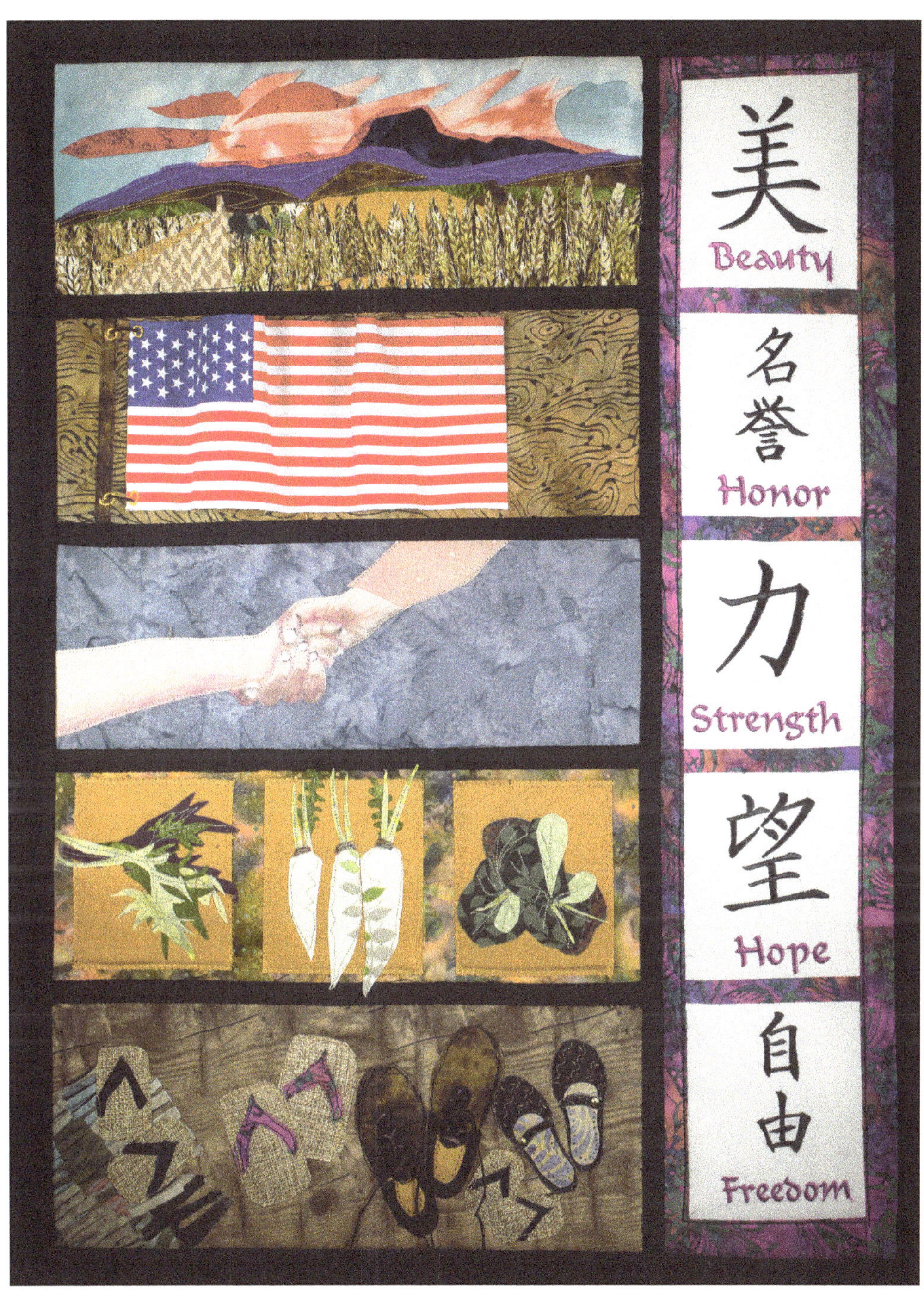

美
Beauty
名誉
Honor
力
Strength
望
Hope
自由
Freedom

"Healing Heart"

Heart Mountain is a landmark that has witnessed both geologic and human events. May its name remind us that only love endures.

Alice Flyr
Cody, Wyoming

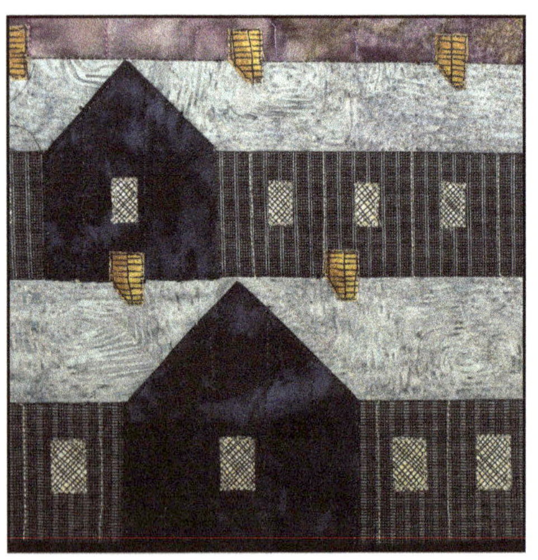

VISITOR COMMENTS:

"Thank you for a wonderful, emotion-stirring, thought-provoking exhibit. Your presence is a jewel on Heart Mountain."

–Anonymous

"As a quilter, this was an art form from beyond. What a beautiful display of the use of hearts and hands."

–Cleo, from Montana

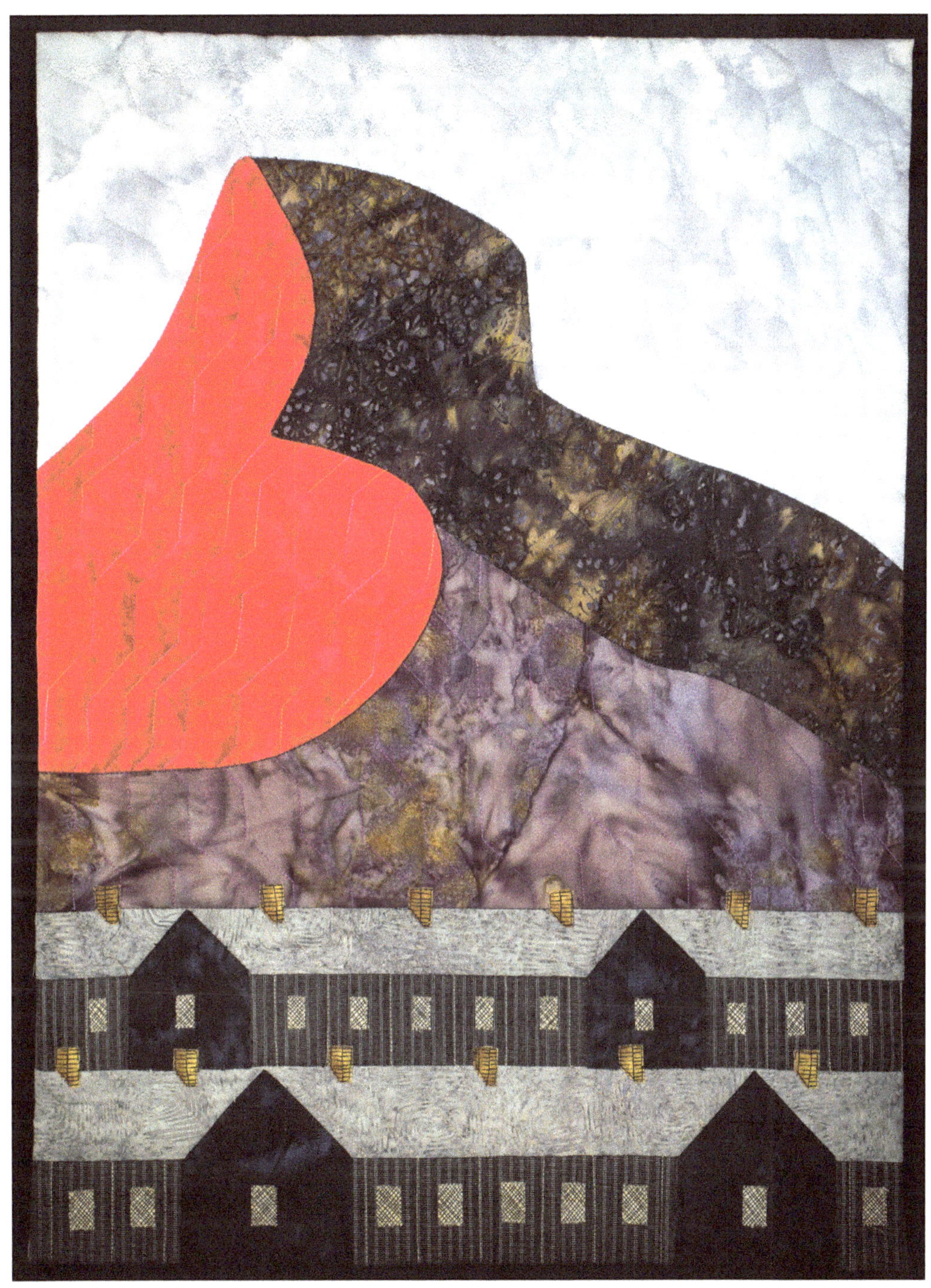

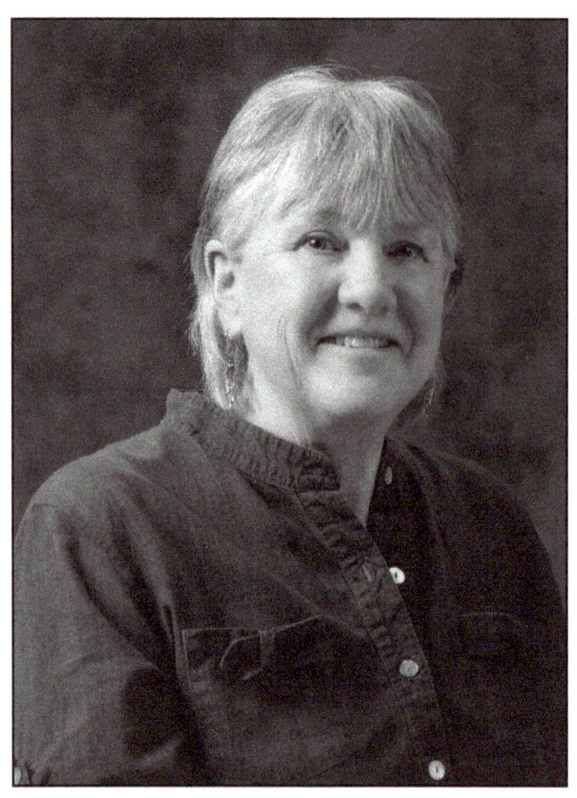

Kathy Hammond
Thermopolis, Wyoming

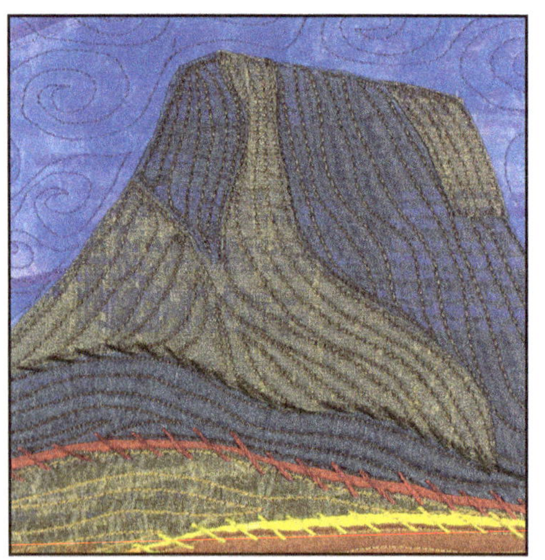

"HEART MOUNTAIN BARRACKS"

The barracks are gone, but the lessons of what we learned from this portion of our history need to continue. The Heart Mountain Interpretive Center has helped us to remember these lessons of treating each other with respect and dignity and to overcome our fears so that horrible situations are not created again.

This quilt was made with silk (commercially woven, hand dyed and silk scraps from kimonos). Threads are cotton, silk and rayon. Documents from the Santa Fe Internment Camp are silk screened onto the quilt.

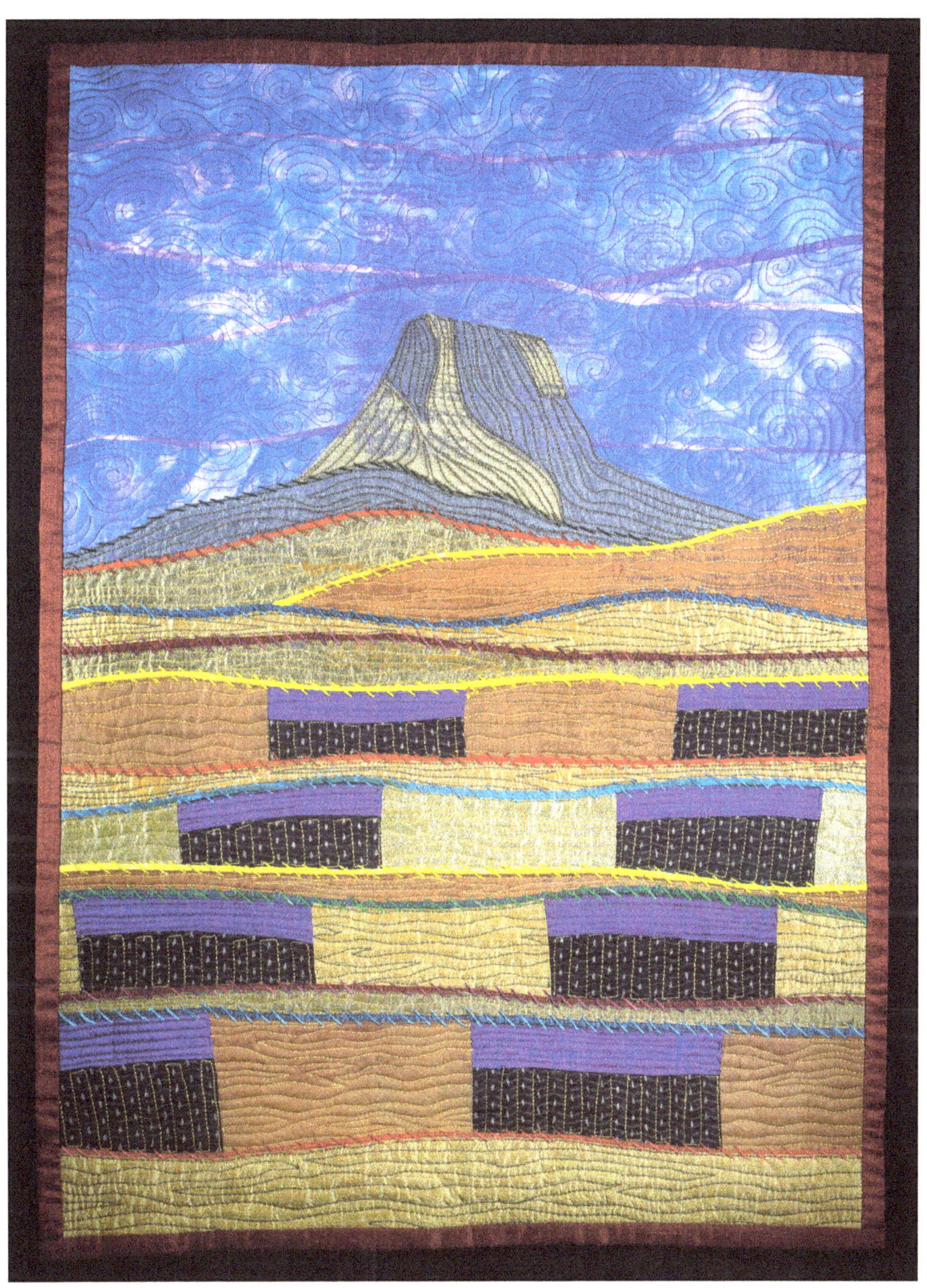

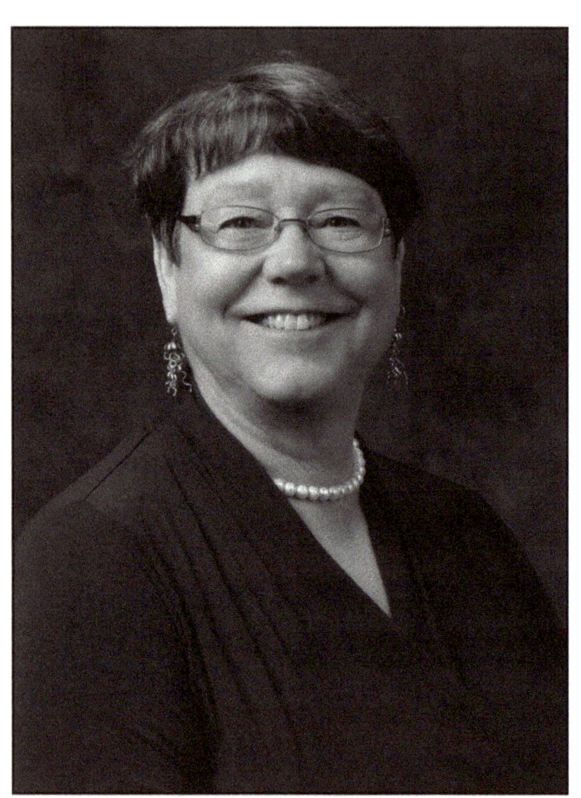

Pam Harris
Cody, Wyoming

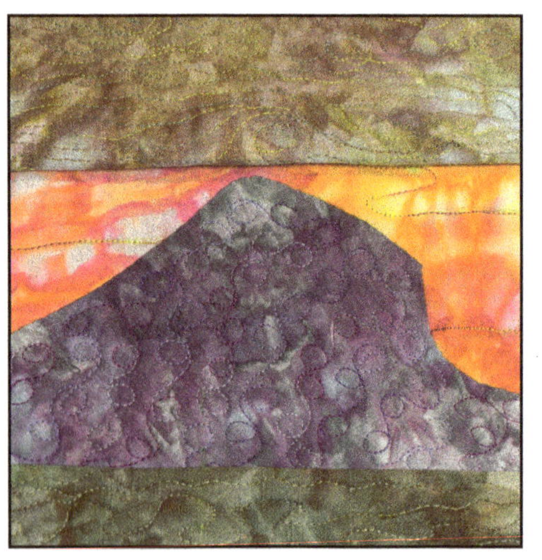

"Heart Mountain Harvest"

The root cellar vents are monuments to phenomenal agricultural accomplishments.

Ice dyed fabrics represent earth, water, sun and the wide variety of crops including some that had never been grown in the region.

Visitor Comments:

"I am awestruck at the creativity and skill of all the women's quilting. This exhibit should travel throughout the U.S. and Wyoming."

–Anonymous

"Gorgeous. Stunning. I have tears in my eyes—the beauty of the human spirit."

–Norma, from Montana

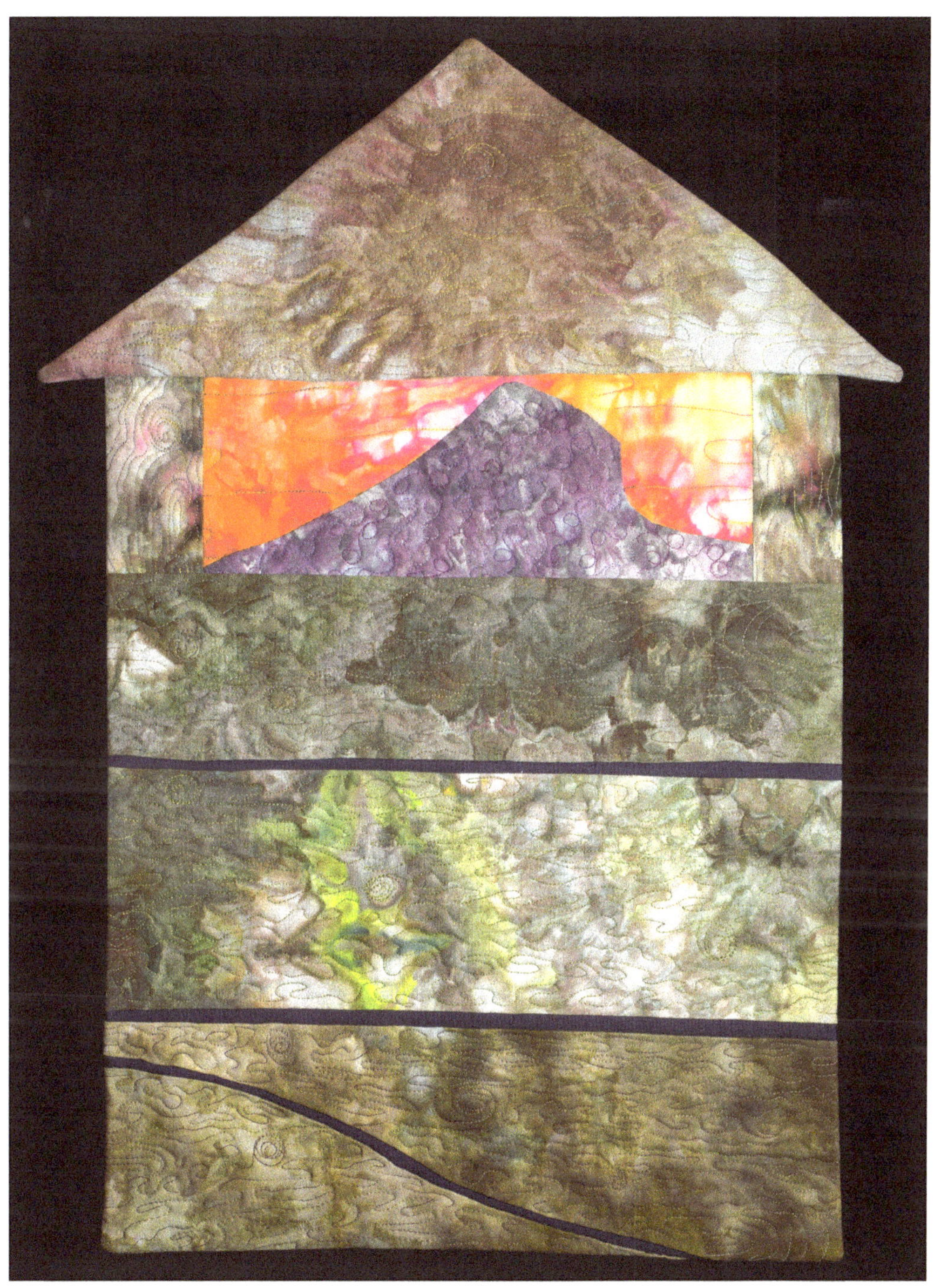

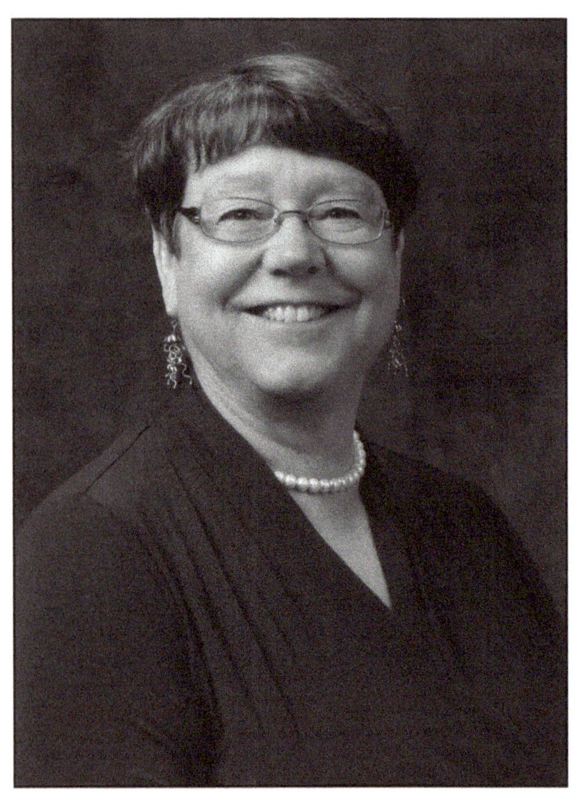

Pam Harris
Cody, Wyoming

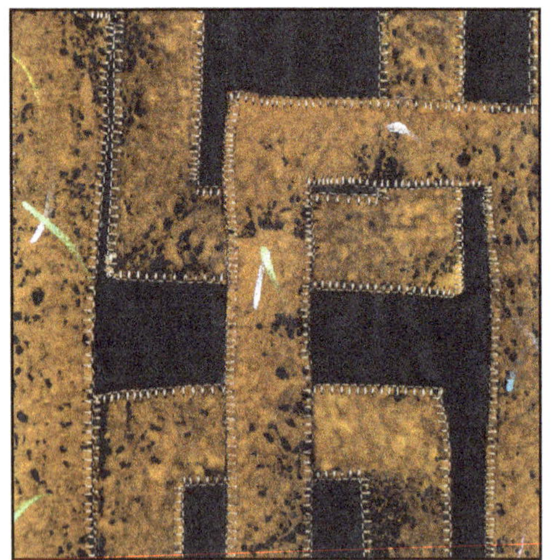

"What is Your Barrack Number?"

Merriam Webster defines 'barrack' as:

A. housing characterized by extreme plainness or dreary uniformity
B. a structure resembling a shed or barn that provides temporary housing

I was moved by how stark, cramped, bleak and open the barracks were. They were hastily constructed with black tar paper and wood that soon cracked allowing the cold air to flow through. The interior walls were all open at the top and the only privacy was the use of curtains.

My quilt portrays my interpretation of lines of drafty, overcrowded, sub-par barracks but also the ways the Japanese Americans made the spaces their own with splashes of color. Black fabric was bleach discharged (brown) with a sponge to achieve an open, airy look. The sponge was flexible so not all the rectangles are straight. Rectangles were cut out, fused to batting and layered.

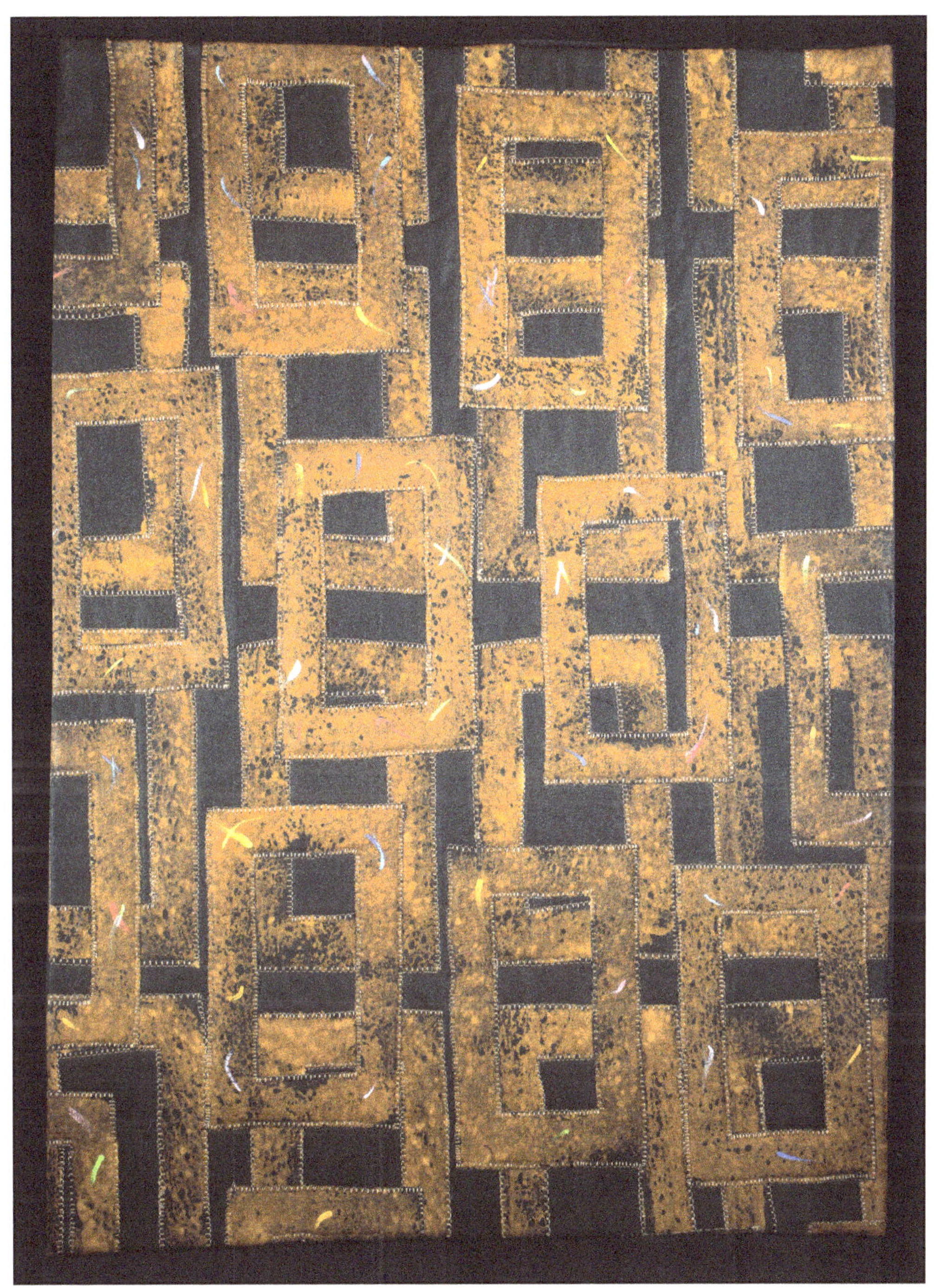

"Gone But Not Forgotten"

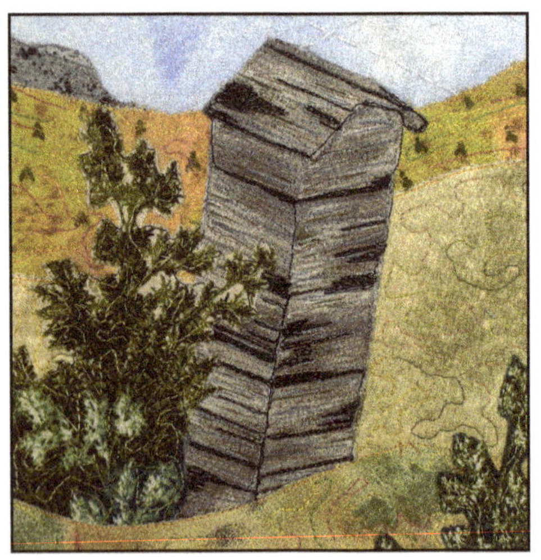

Barbara Harrison
Cody, Wyoming

My quilt depicts the aging vents on the underground food storage "building." It struck me as being a huge undertaking to build such a large food storage area.

The Japanese Americans must have grown an immense amount of food to fill this area up to feed them through the winter. These ingenious people worked very hard to make a bad situation as comfortable as possible.

The quilting techniques used on my quilt are fused, raw edge appliqué, lots of thread painting with mostly variegated threads, and both hand and machine quilting.

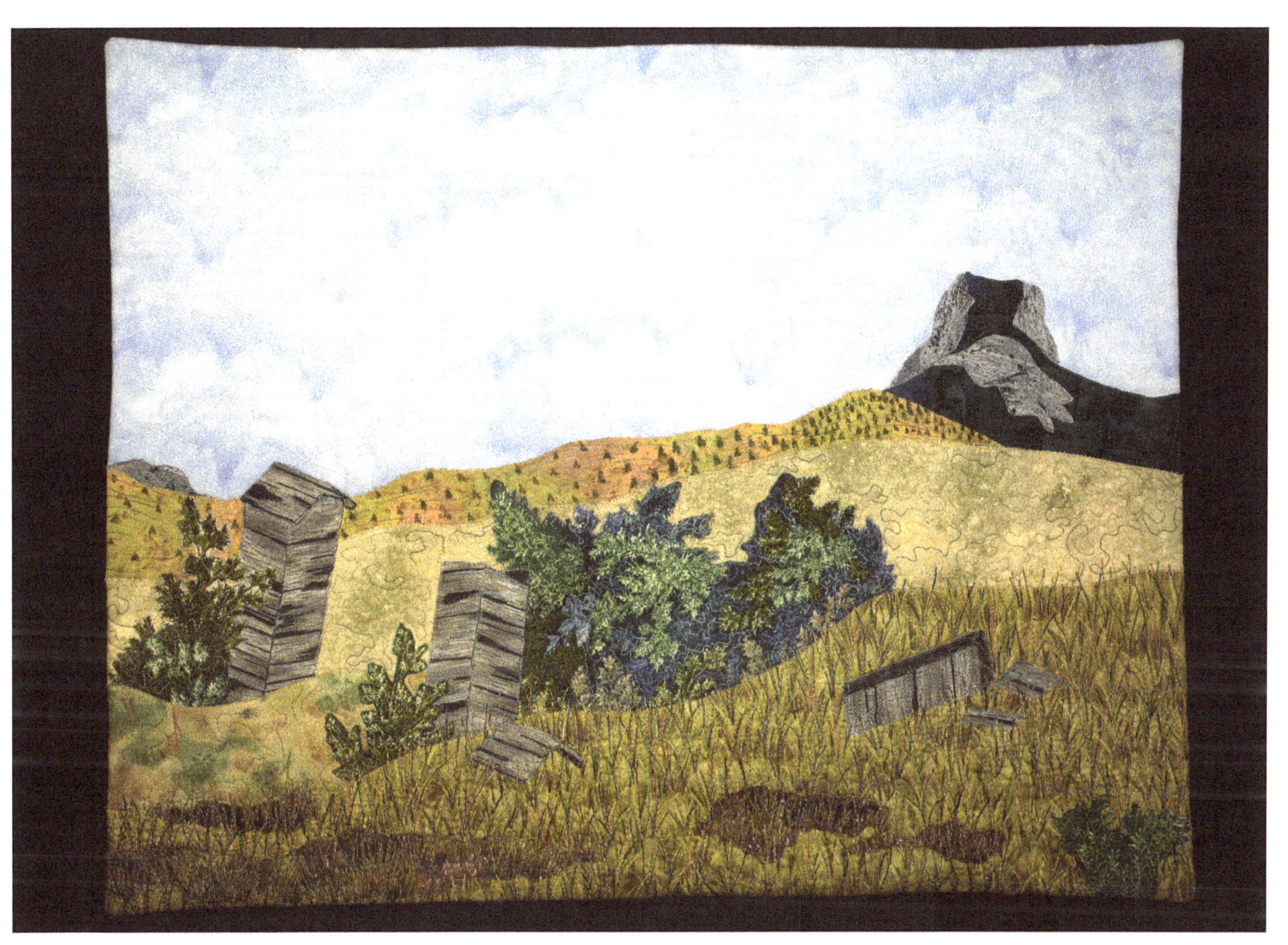

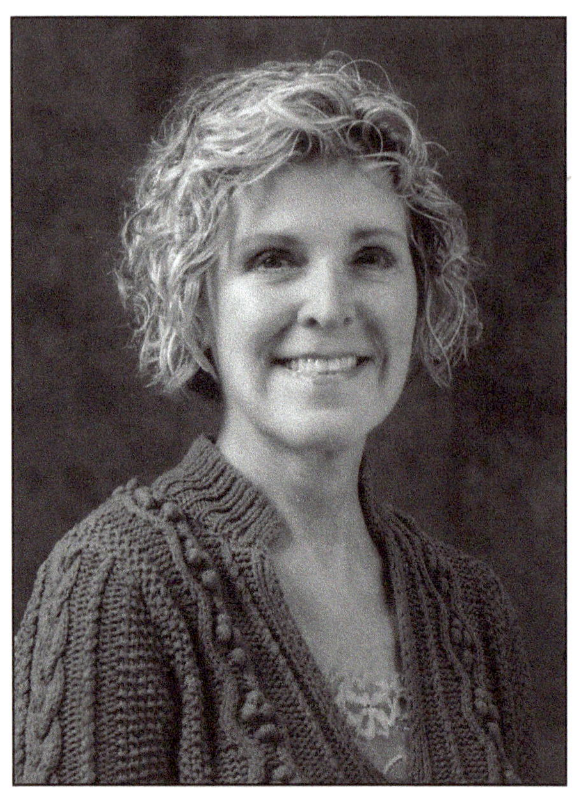

Jan Hoar
Cody, Wyoming

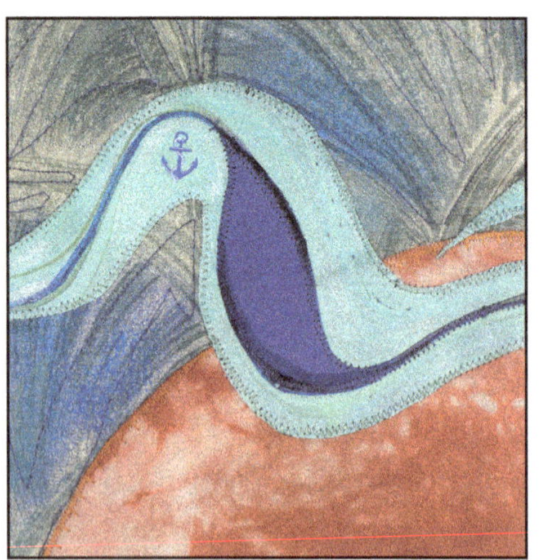

"NIDOTO NAI YONI"

My quilt is a timeline: The 1941 bombing of Pearl Harbor is the oil spill at the top of the quilt. (Two to nine quarts per day still seep from the wreckage of the USS Arizona.) The subsequent 1942 internment of Japanese Americans is represented by buttons (people) being railroaded through an angry and confused orange world and into a dark hole/barracks.

The freeing of Japanese Americans from Heart Mountain Internment Camp in 1945 is represented by the scattering of buttons and celebratory yarn. They are going home. The USA apologized to these Japanese Americans in 1988. 知恵 Wisdom (finally)!

I created this quilt with Shibori dyed fabric, photo art, and acrylic paint on fabric, yarn, and buttons.

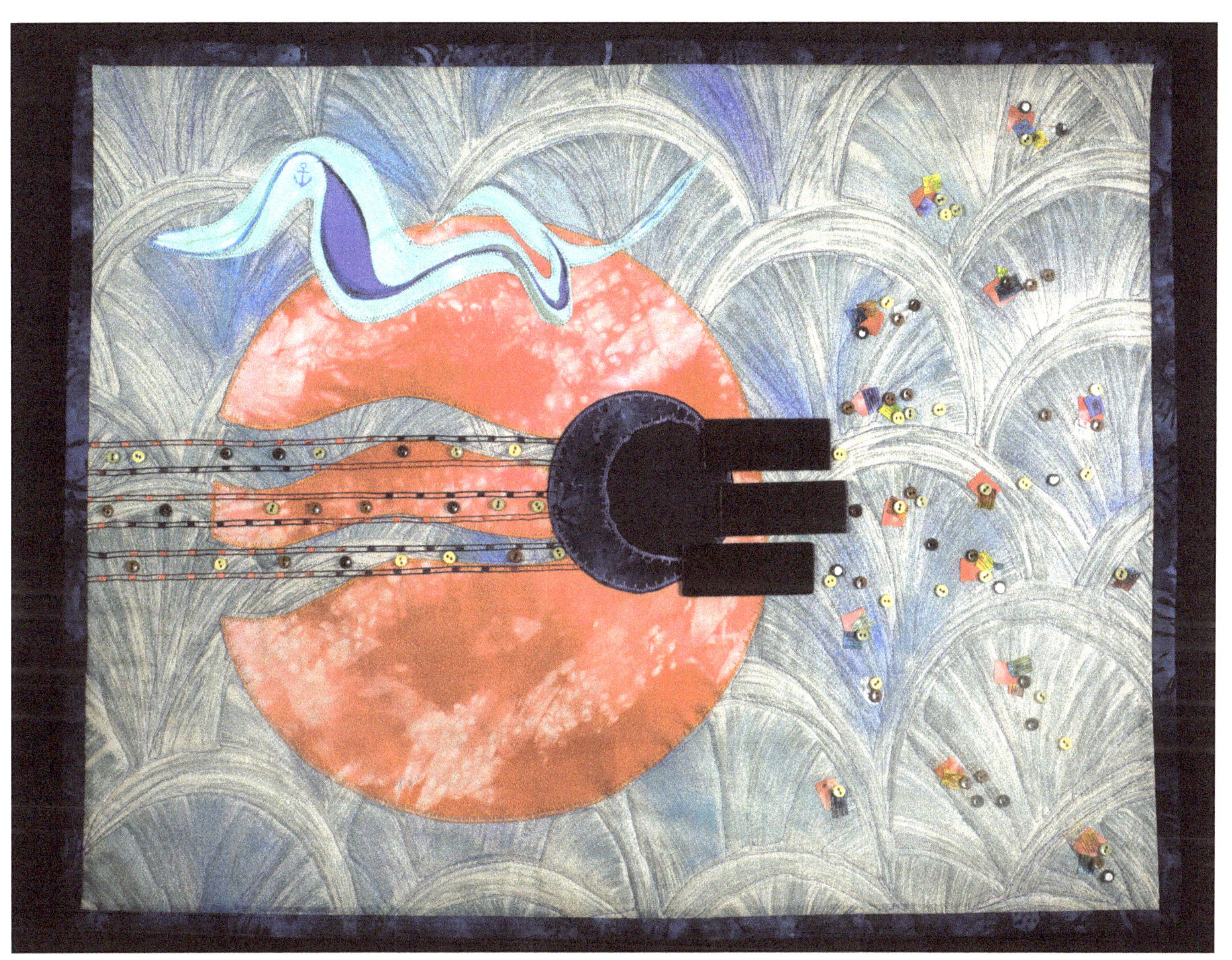

"ONE SUITCASE"

Carol Kolf
Sheridan, Wyoming

In 1942 Franklin D. Roosevelt signed Executive Order 9066, which resulted in "exclusion zones" where U.S. citizens of Japanese ancestry were to be removed. This ultimately led to the incarceration of 120,000 Japanese Americans.

These American citizens with Japanese ancestry were allowed to fill ONE SUITCASE when they were taken from their homes, their jobs, their possessions and their businesses and brought to an unknown place with meager accommodations.

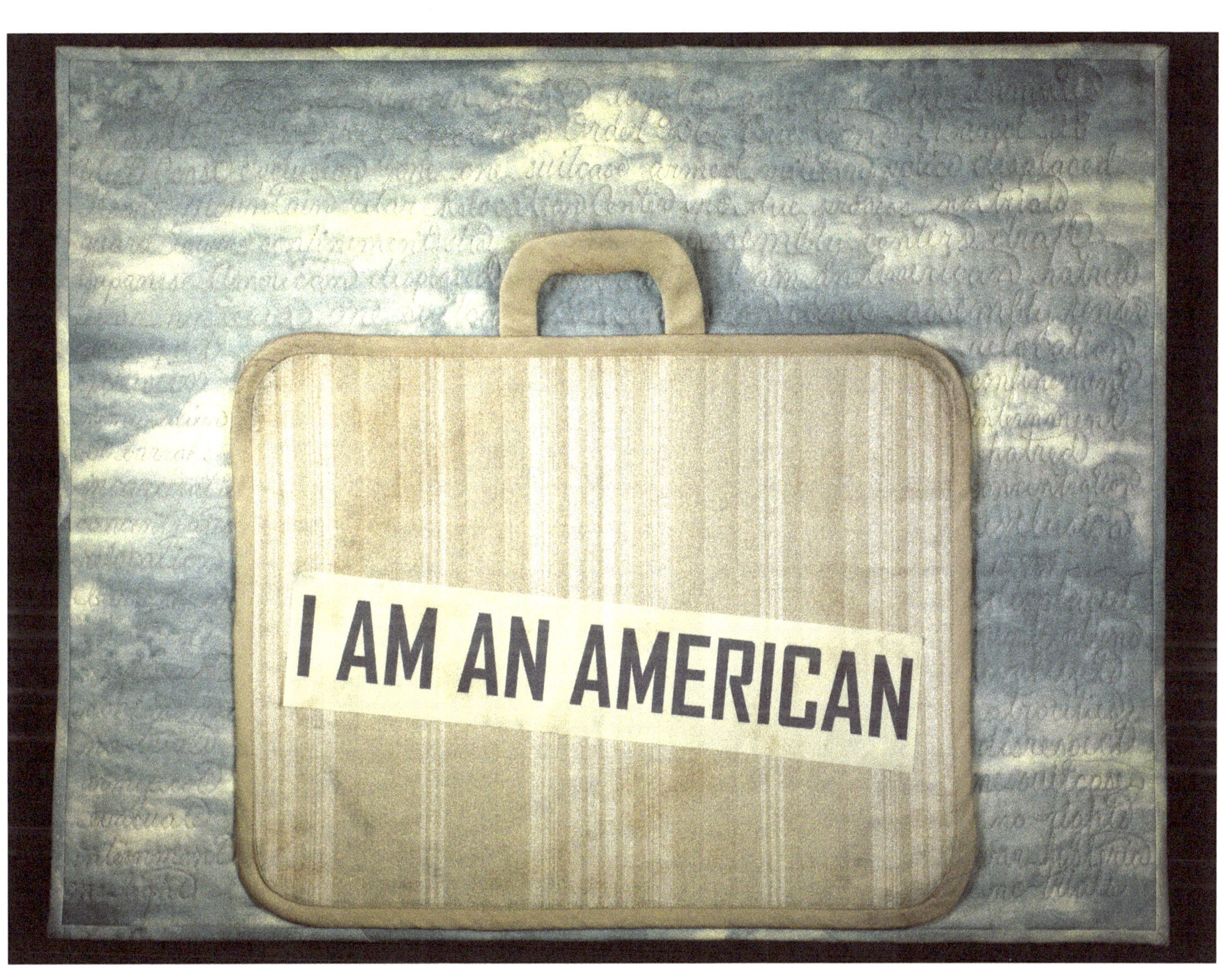
I AM AN AMERICAN

"Heart Mountain 1942"

I chose to do my impression of the mountain. It can be seen from nearly everywhere we look in Cody and Powell, Wyoming. I have always thought of Heart Mountain as beautiful.

In 1942 it became the site of the Heart Mountain Internment Camp. As a prison for 14,025 Japanese Americans, this camp was the third largest town in Wyoming before it was closed November 10, 1945. I wonder in the political climate of this day could this shame of 1942 happen again?

Jeanne Knudsen
Cody, Wyoming

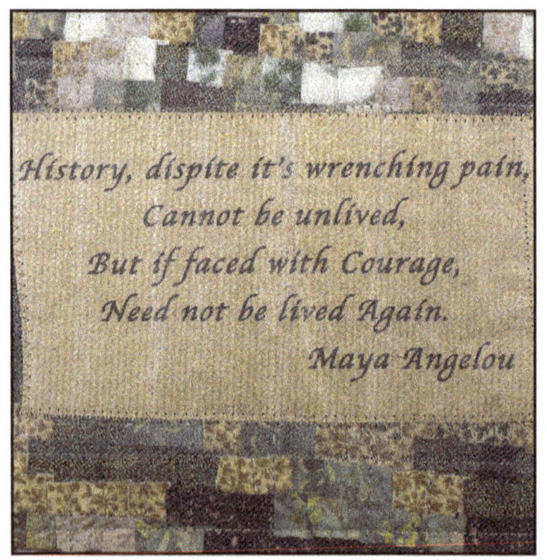

Visitor Comments:

"These quilts are beautiful and stark. They evoked raw sadness and fear. Beautiful, thank you."

–Kelly, from Montana

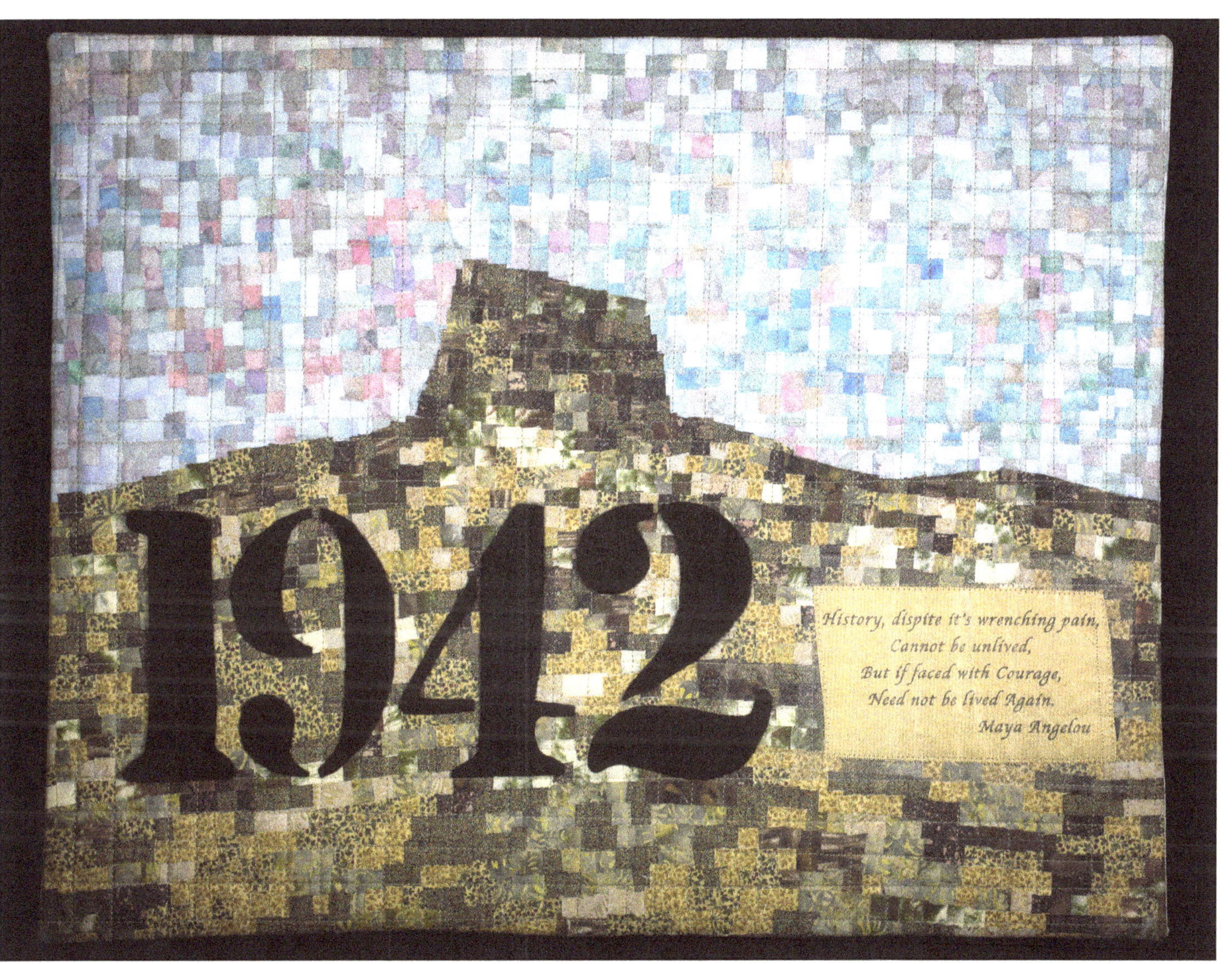

1942
History, dispite it's wrenching pain,
Cannot be unlived,
But if faced with Courage,
Need not be lived Again.
Maya Angelou

"The Children"

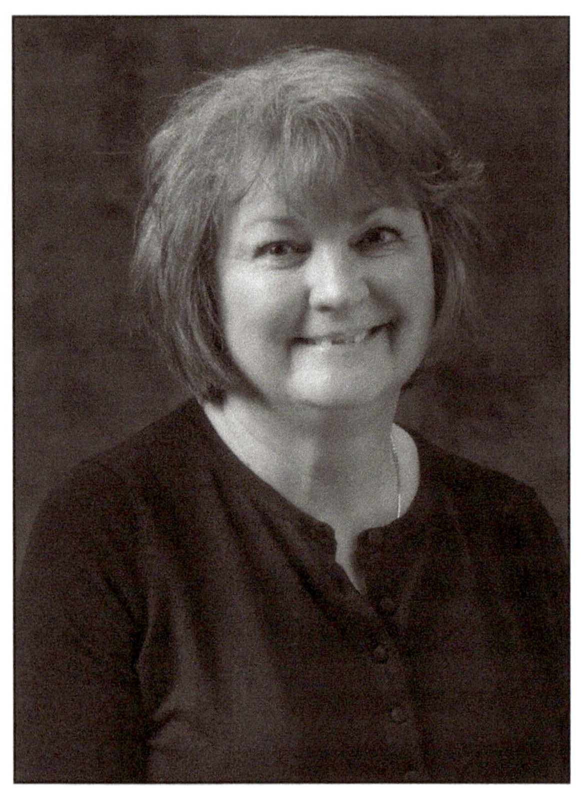

Jeanne Knudsen
Cody, Wyoming

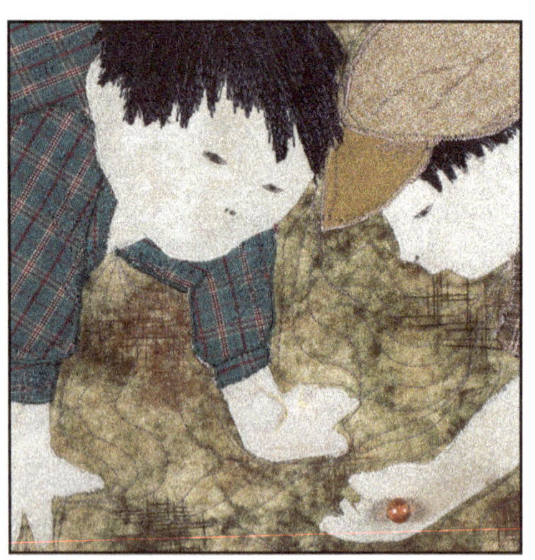

About 120,000 Japanese Americans were imprisoned during World War II under Executive Order 9066. Half of them were children. It is heartbreaking to imagine how "Mother" and "Father" felt not knowing where they would be sent, what the conditions would be, would the children stay with them or be separated. I imagine there was a lot of worry and concern for the family.

Many of the photos at Heart Mountain Interpretive Center are of the children. Although the circumstances were extremely hard for anyone imprisoned illegally, I found that in many of the photos the children are playing baseball, marbles, running and doing schoolwork. I wanted to show that side of the camp in my art. The children of these camps are now grown. Many have had very successful lives. And that, reminds me of a quote:

> *Hardships often prepare*
> *Ordinary people for*
> *Extraordinary destiny.*
>
> **–C.S. Lewis**

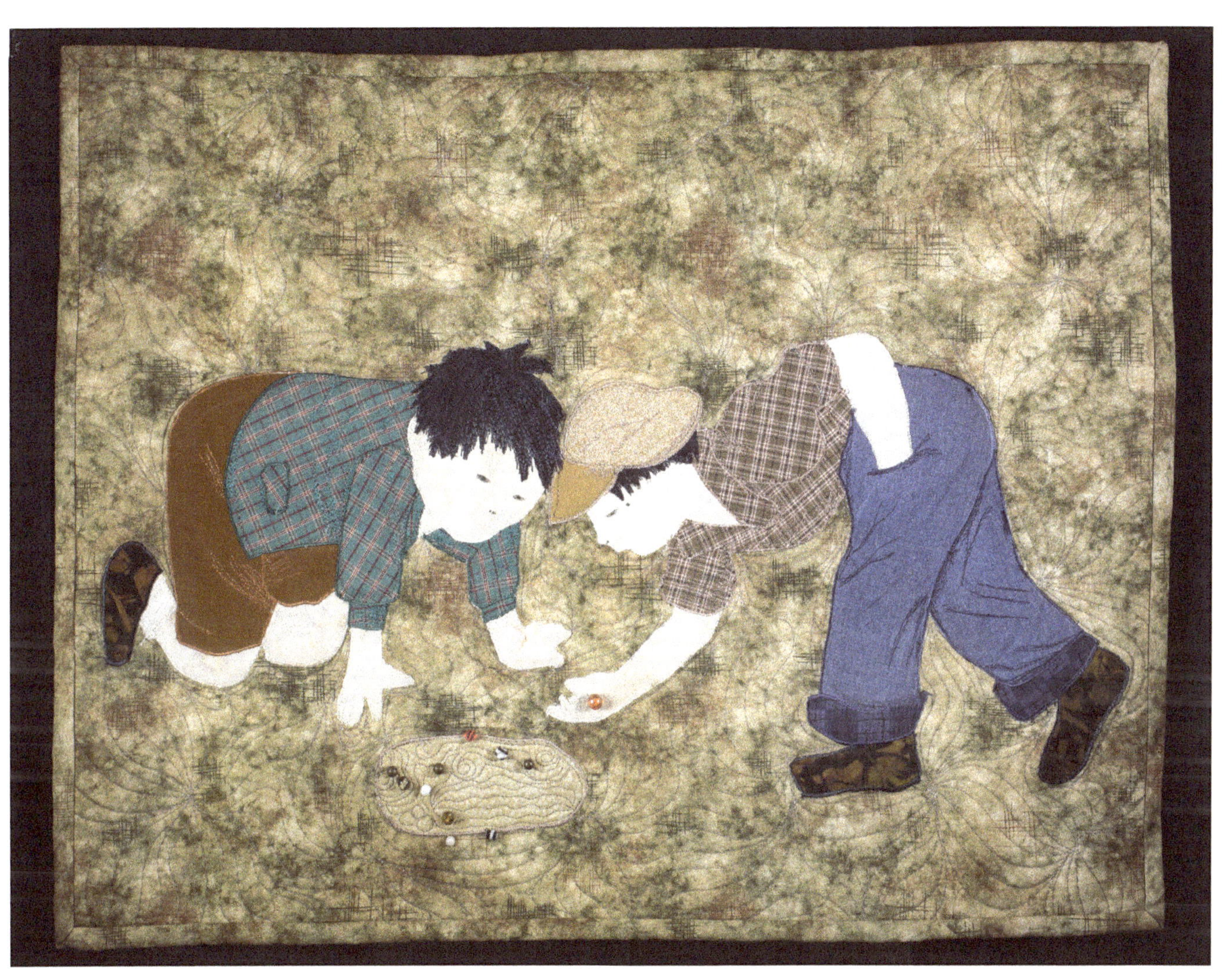

"...AND THE WIND BLOWS"

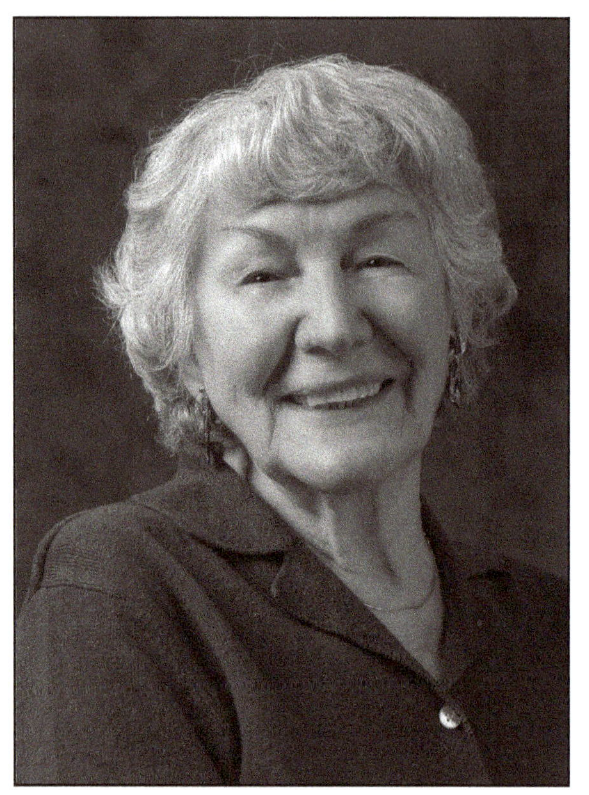

Pat Larsen
Powell, Wyoming

Moving here from California I became acutely aware of the difference in climate. After visiting Heart Mountain Internment Camp site I could empathize with the adjustments and hardships the internees had to endure.

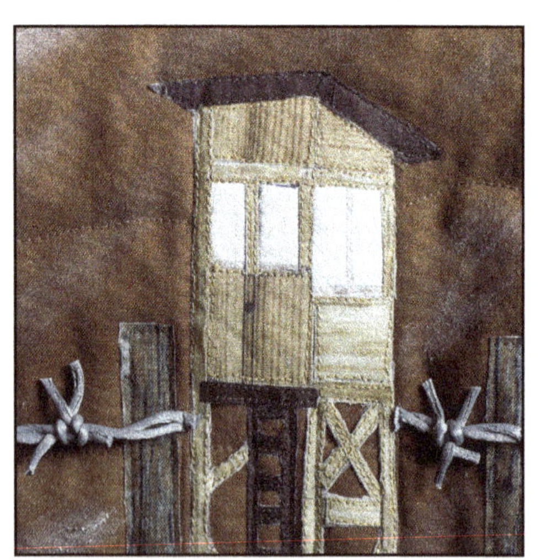

VISITOR COMMENTS:

"Wonderful exhibit. Loved the expressions of the emotions of history in fabric and texture. The 'relocated' native tribes in Alaska have used their cultural art to do the same thing to help heal."

–Julieann, from Alaska

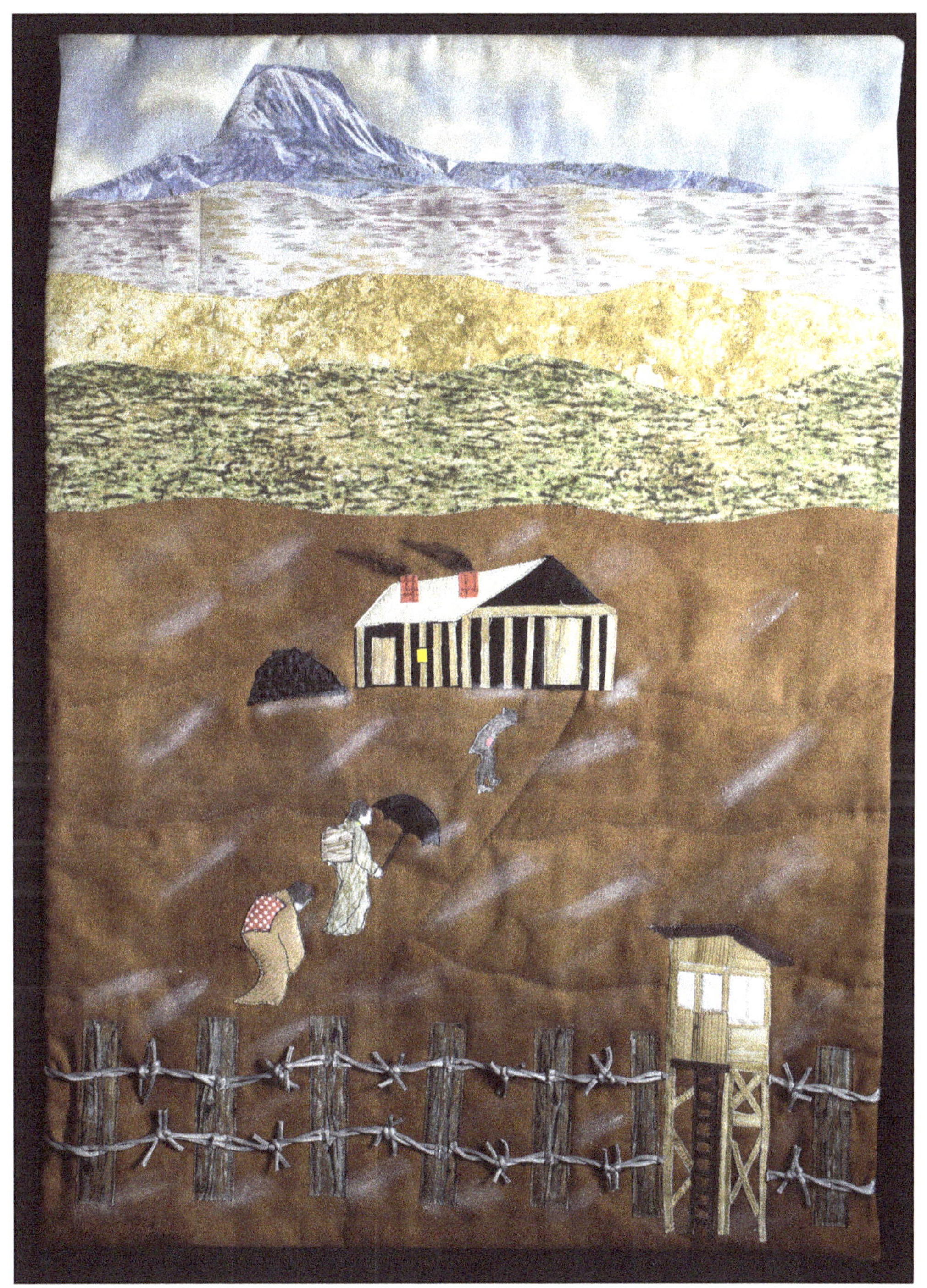

"Daily Chores"

My inspiration for this piece is the human spirit and how we can make the best of any situation. As detainees adjusted to their new life at Heart Mountain, they continued their daily chores, including wash day and gardening. They built raised containers for vegetables on the hillside and raised crops on the flats. These farming techniques were so successful that their crops supplied other relocation camps with fresh foods as well.

The clothes drying in the breeze are made from actual Japanese kimono scraps.

Linda MacDonald
Powell, Wyoming

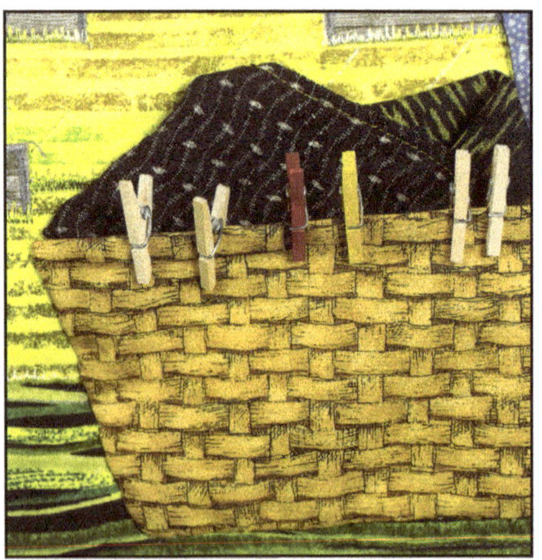

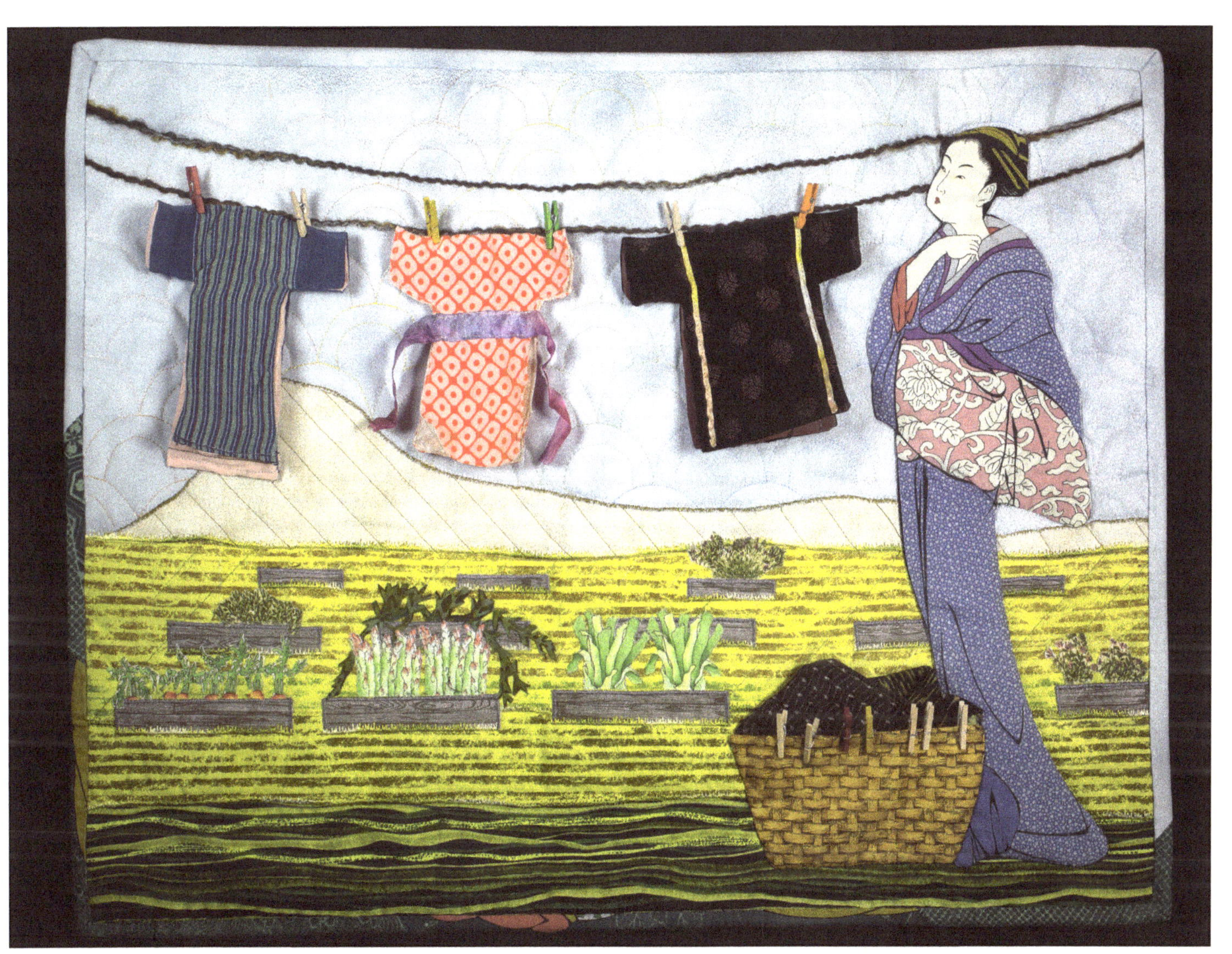

"ENDURANCE"

The historical hospital boiler house with its towering red chimney still stands like a beacon today at the Heart Mountain historic site. It is a landmark that can be seen when traveling Highway 14A between Cody and Powell.

The chimney reminds me of the courage and fortitude the Japanese Americans in the camps displayed during WWII. They demonstrated their great strength, despite what they had to endure, even after the end of the war.

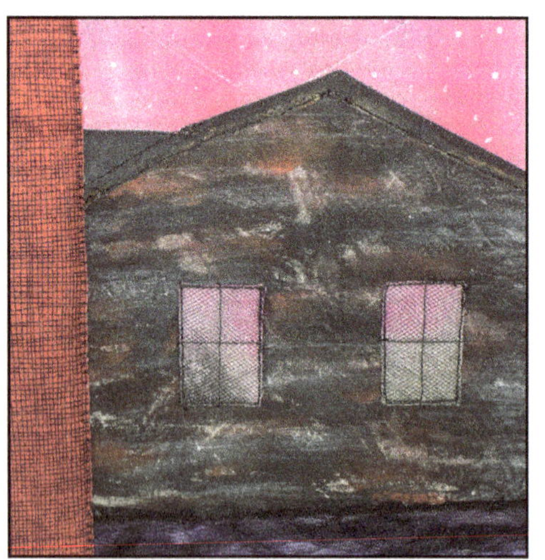

Patty Mayfield
Powell, Wyoming

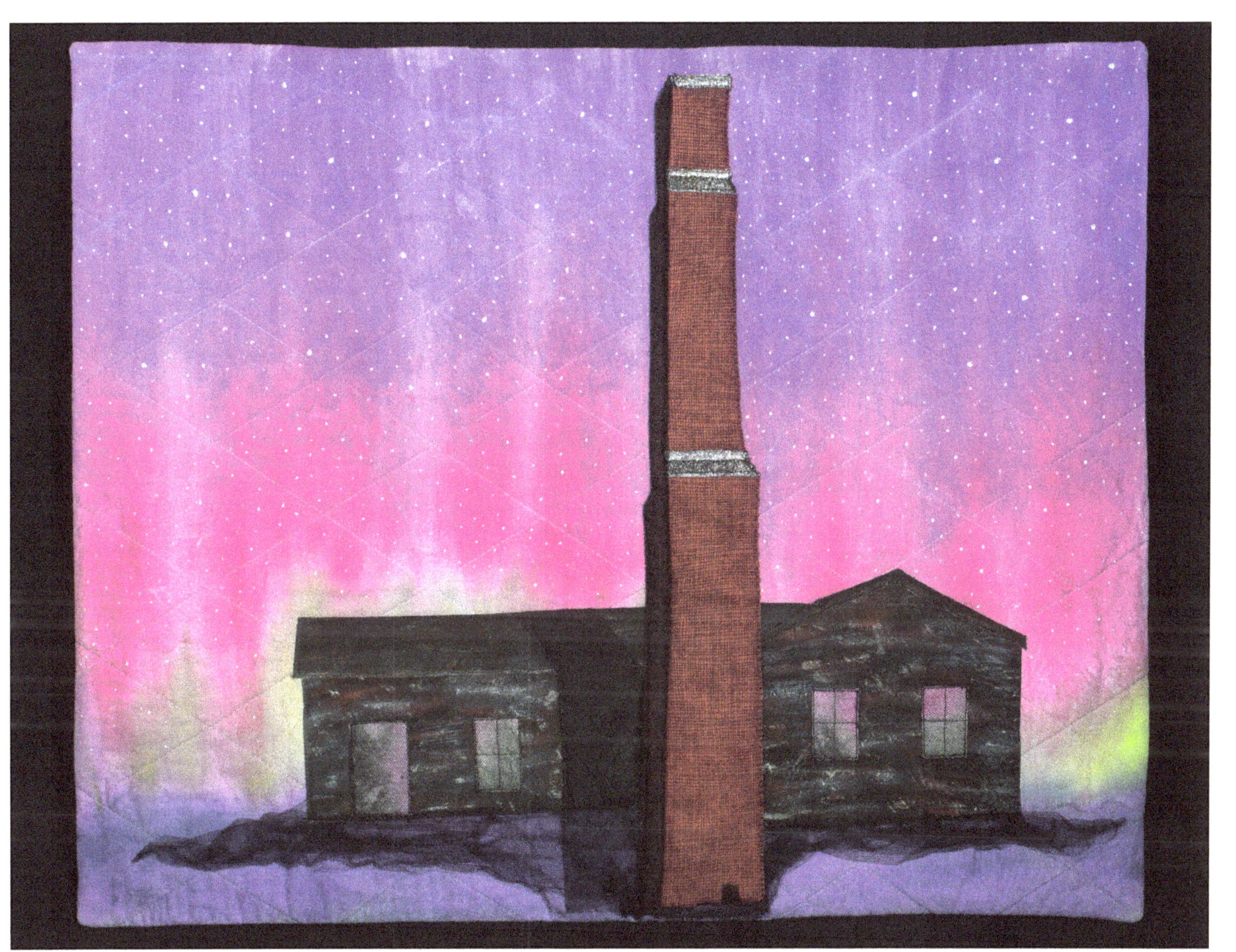

"A City Far Away"

Maybe, looking into the dark sky unencumbered by city lights, the internees could feel a sense of peace as they looked at the Milky Way and Orion on a clear night. The city lights so far in the distance might have reminded them of the places they had to leave behind. How many different thoughts would be in the minds of those 11,000 individuals?

My 18" x 24" quilt is constructed using wool, alpaca roving, commercial fabric, and netting. It is machine quilted and hand beaded.

Marybeth Richardson
Powell, Wyoming

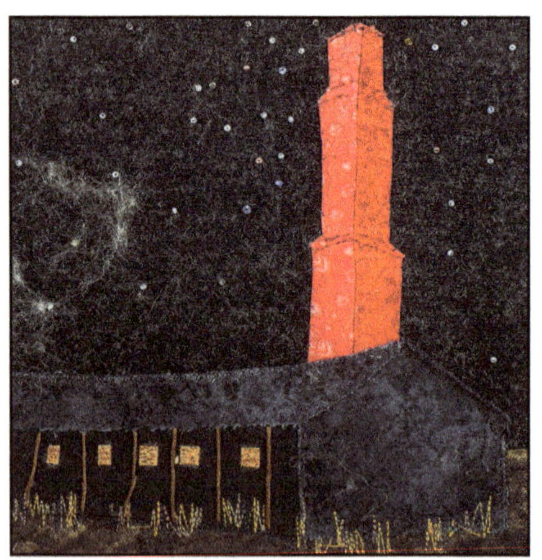

VISITOR COMMENTS:

"The variety of expressions by the quilters speaks to the vibrancy of artists responding to one creative spark: Japanese American internment. Outstanding!"

–Gayle, from Iowa

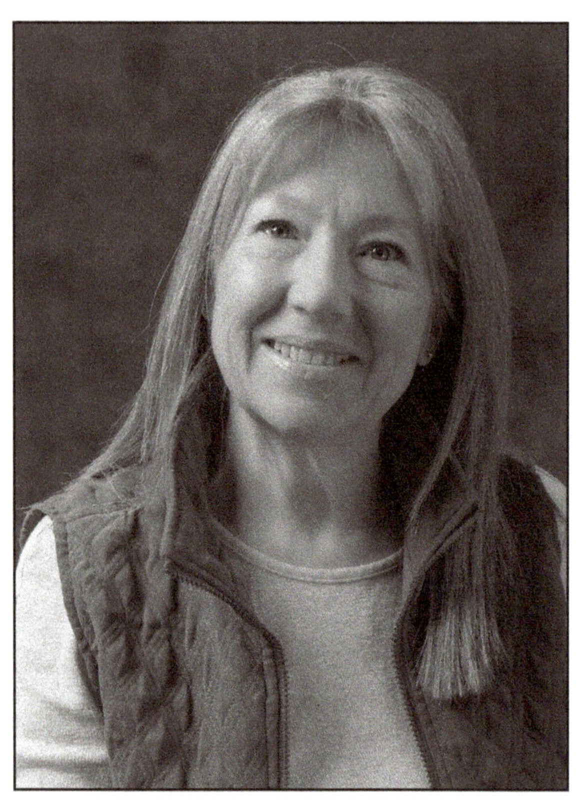

Rebecca True
Cody, Wyoming

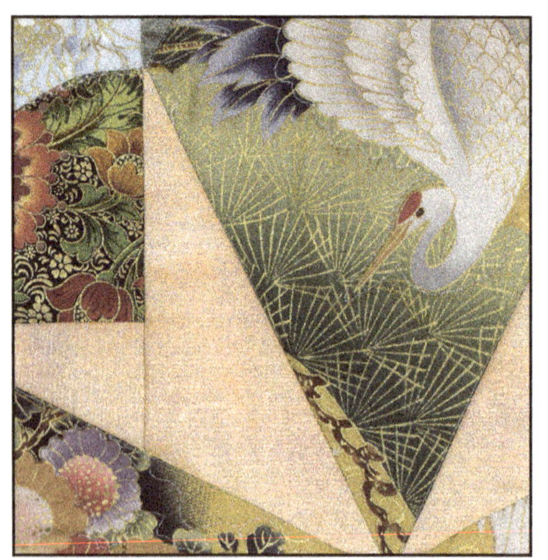

"Three Quilts Tell the Story: Before, During and After Executive Order 9066"

I began this artistic expression by constructing three identical quilts.

Quilt #1: "BEFORE Executive Order 9066"

Silk and cotton fabrics in tea green and melon colors are pieced on a field of blue sky. Cranes traditionally represent long life and good luck. I left this quilt intact to represent the rich culture and beauty of Japanese American lives before Executive Order 9066.

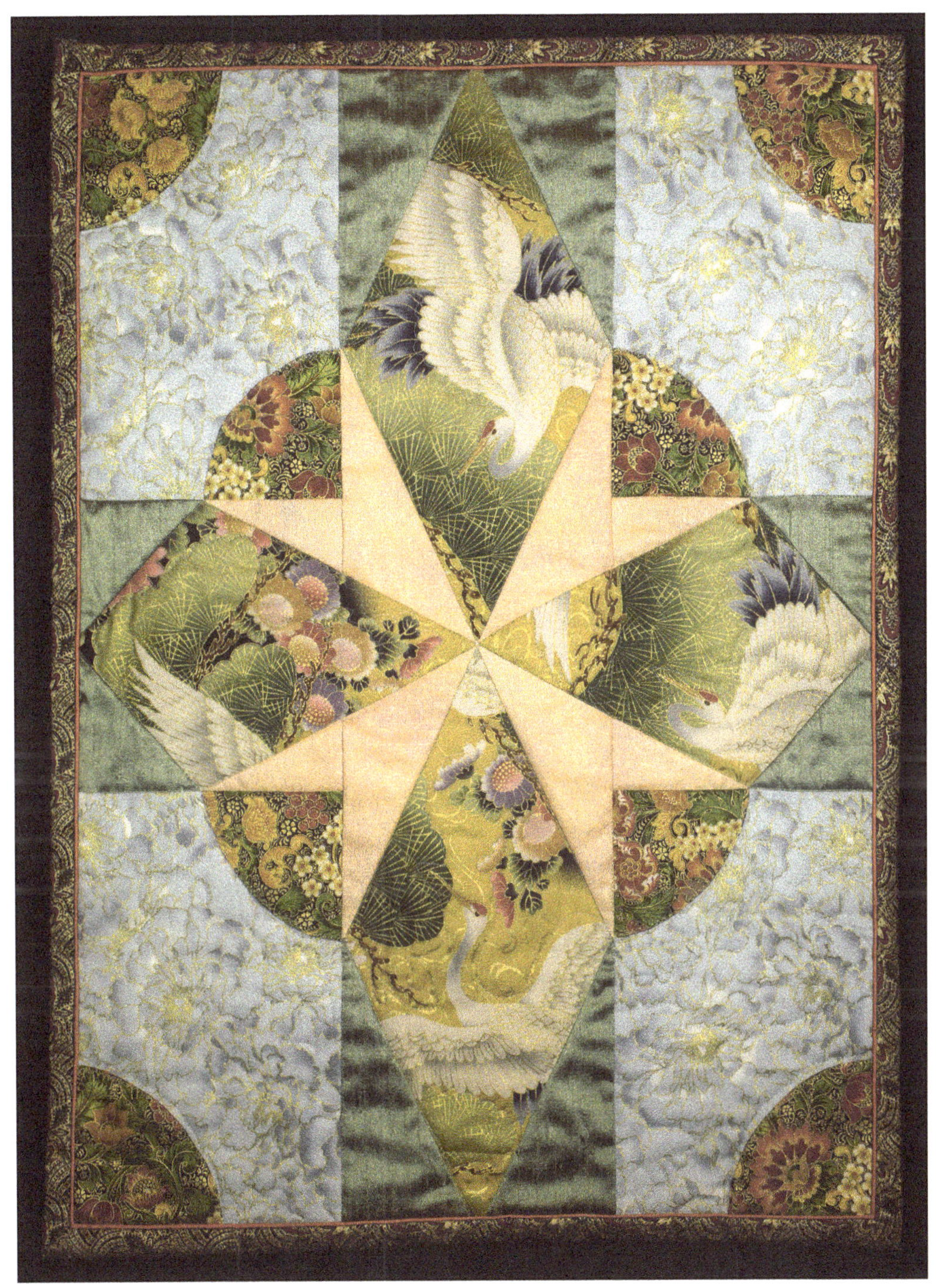

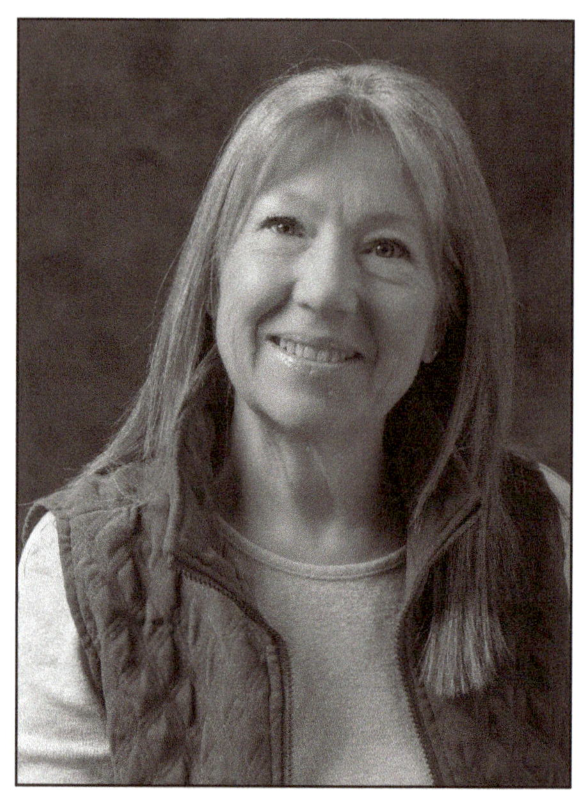

Rebecca True
Cody, Wyoming

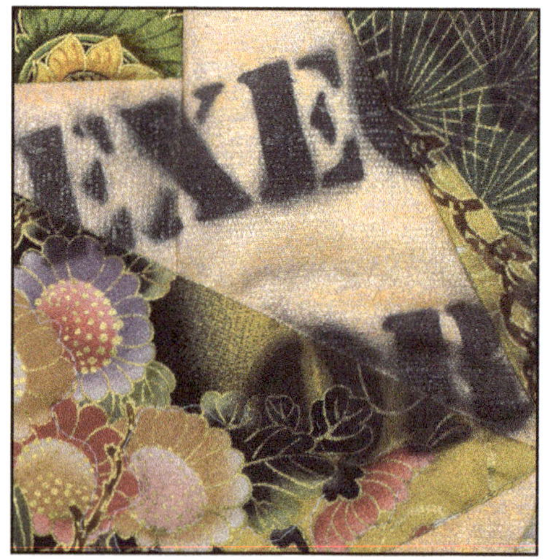

QUILT #2: "DURING EXECUTIVE ORDER 9066"

The fabric of life for 120,000 Japanese Americans was changed forever once the ink of this black and white rule was applied. To depict these devastating effects, I spray painted this quilt with the words "Executive Order 9066." I then stitched on 3 strands of barbed wire to represent the 3 years that previously productive, colorful lives were denied freedom and restricted behind a barbed wire barrier.

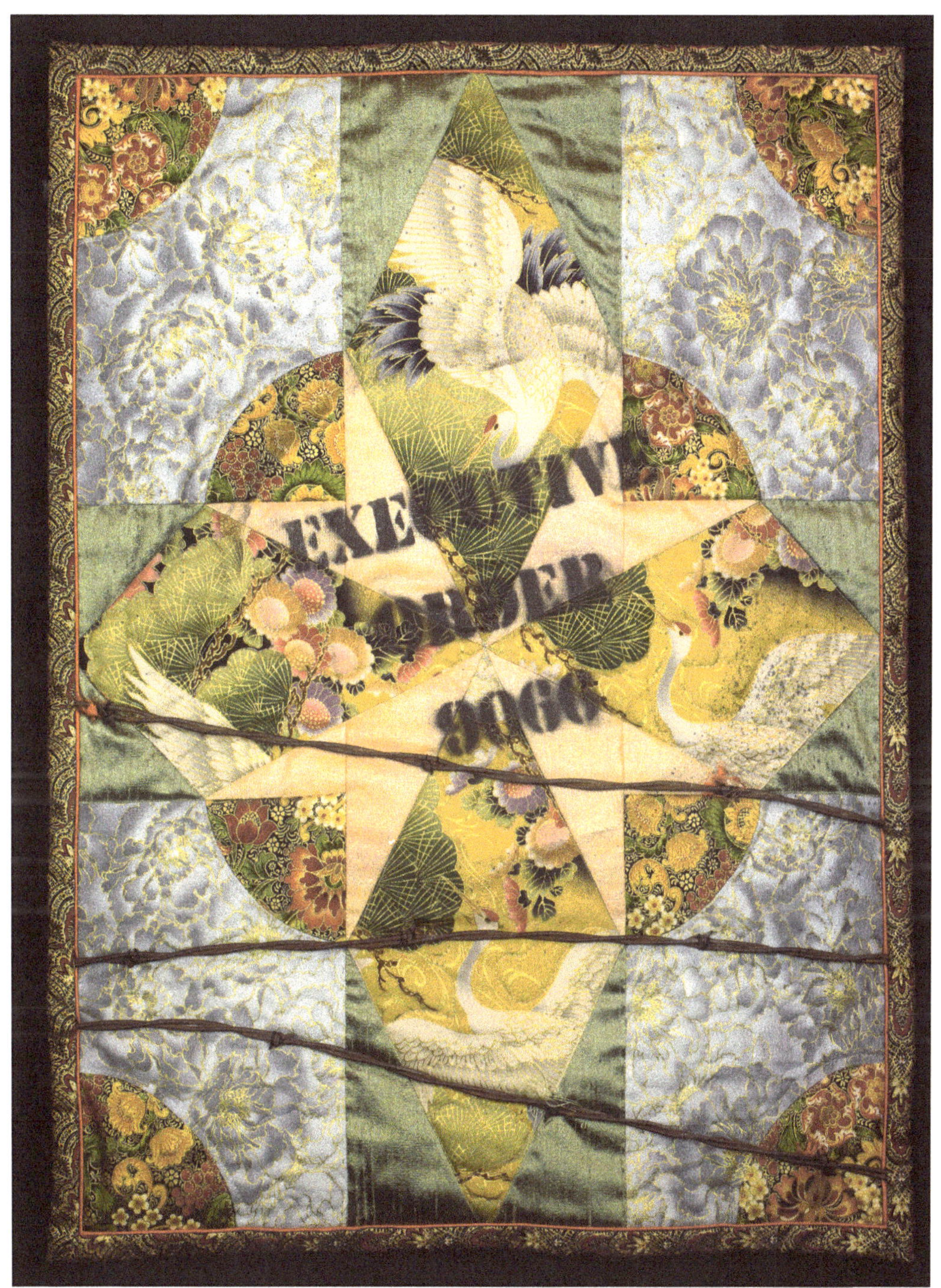
EXECUTIVE
ORDER
9066

QUILT #3: "AFTER EXECUTIVE ORDER 9066"

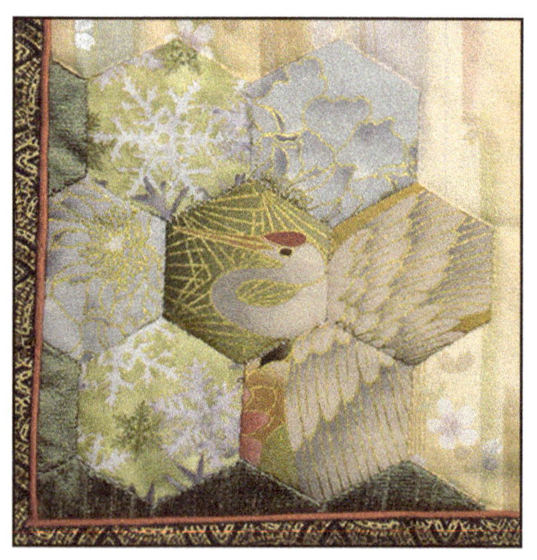

Rebecca True
Cody, Wyoming

First, I spray painted this quilt to be identical to Quilt #2. Then I cut all the seams apart. My goal was to find a way to put the pieces together again, much like the internees had to reconstruct their lives after incarceration and significant losses. Could it be done? Could it be made to look whole, if not beautiful? I trimmed, sorted and turned fabrics over. Some pieces were beyond repair. Others were re-sewn. New fabrics joined paint-stained remnants. In time, a new, vibrant pattern emerged. What also emerged was a deep respect for the discipline, grace, and focus required by the internees to endure the process of their recovery. This quilt honors each of them—those who survived and those who did not. I hope it also inspires a deeper understanding of the sustaining Japanese belief—that the new is made richer because of the old, and that beauty cannot be realized without incorporating the past.

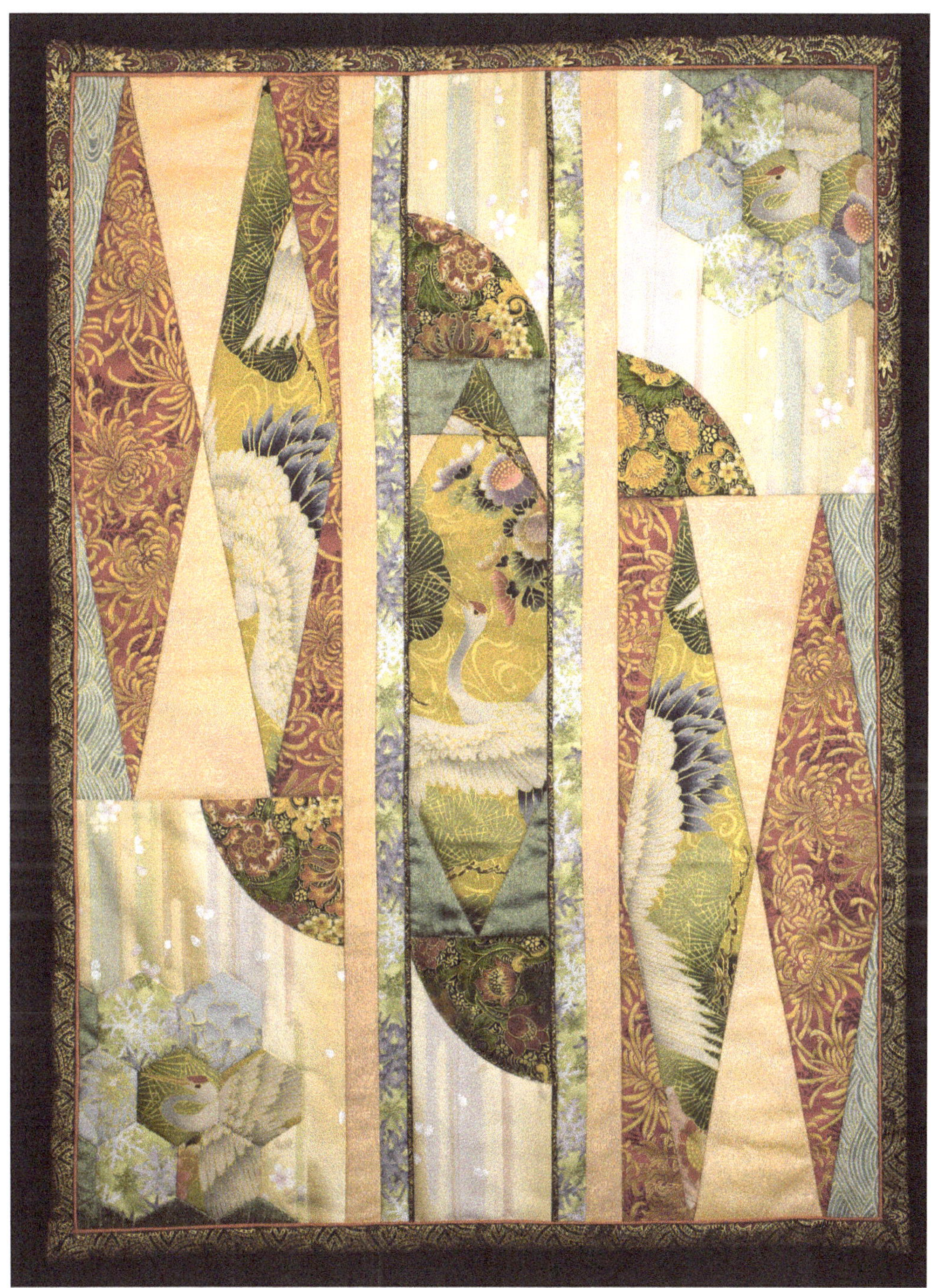

"Maggie and Other Stories"

Making art quilts, with dimensional quality is a creative process I enjoy. Engaging the viewer to explore what lies hidden within the quilt story is my goal. In this quilt, a collage style was used to portray a few stories that touch and haunt the soul.

Lili Turnell
Meeteetse, Wyoming

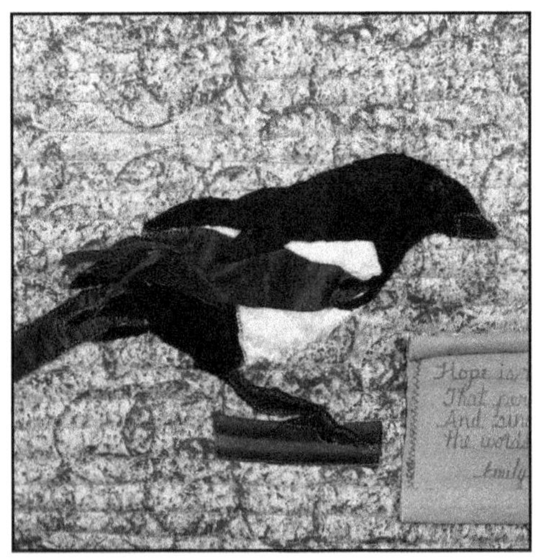

VISITOR COMMENTS:

"Each quilt is a story in itself. They are so unique and really provide inspiration for thinking about our lives and history."

–Donna, from Montana

"Really gorgeous quilts. I've never seen anything like them. Amazing."

–Reagan, from Missouri

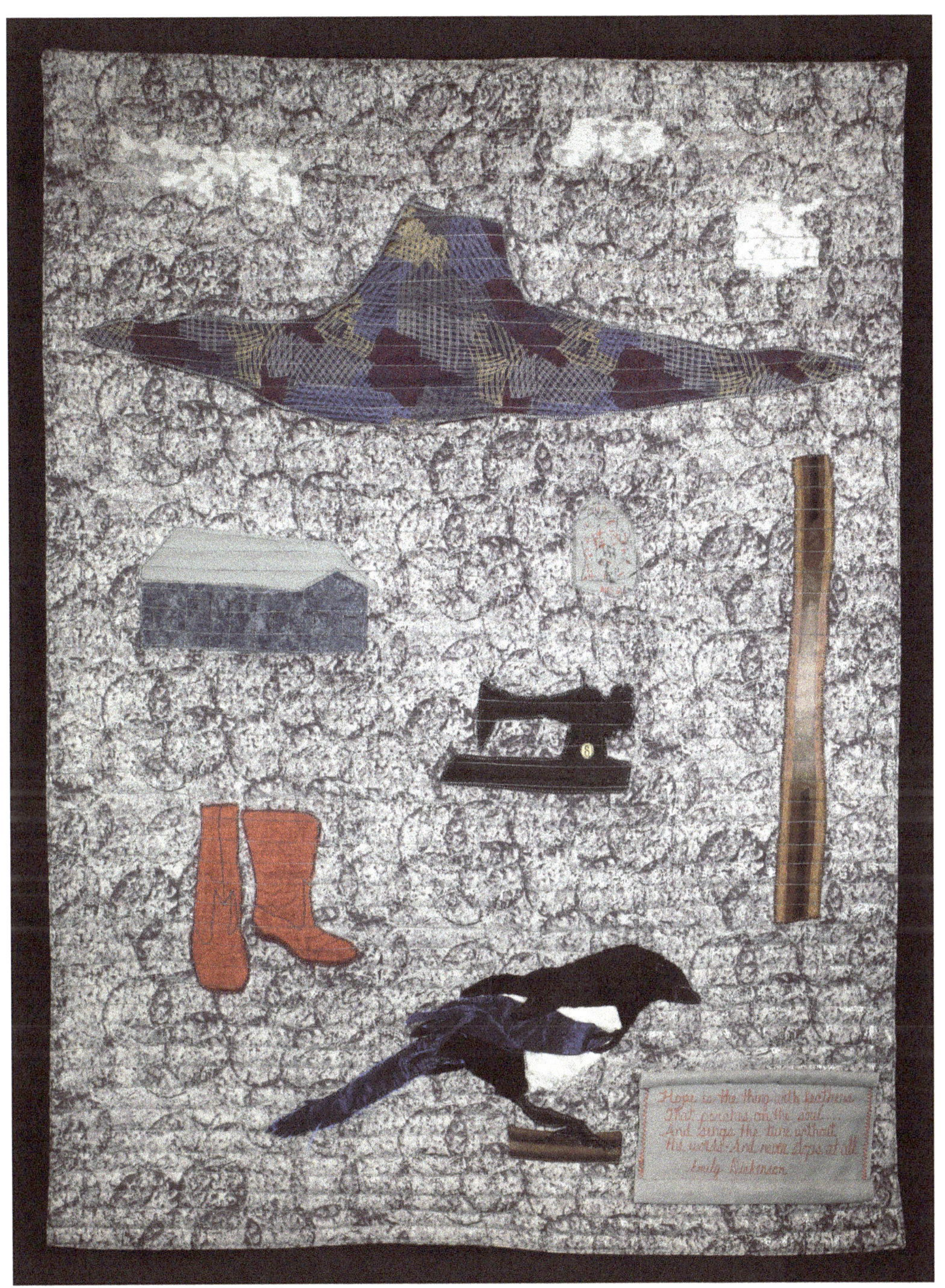
Hope is the thing with feathers
That perches on the soul,
And sings the tune without
the words, And never stops at all.
Emily Dickinson

"Only What You Can Carry"

E ach time I've visited the Heart Mountain Interpretive Center, the piles of luggage in various locations in the museum have remained in my thoughts. "Only what you can carry" echoes in my mind as I consider the limited time the internees had to make important decisions with very little information about the future.

They had no idea of what lay ahead. I wonder what they chose to pack without knowing where they were going or how long they would be away from home. Each person was given a tag listing their family name & number. In addition to these, I've added their barrack assignment on the back of each tag on my art quilt.

I think about what I would take. Keepsakes? Extra clothing? Important documents? What would you choose to carry in your bag if you had to leave home for an undetermined place and time?

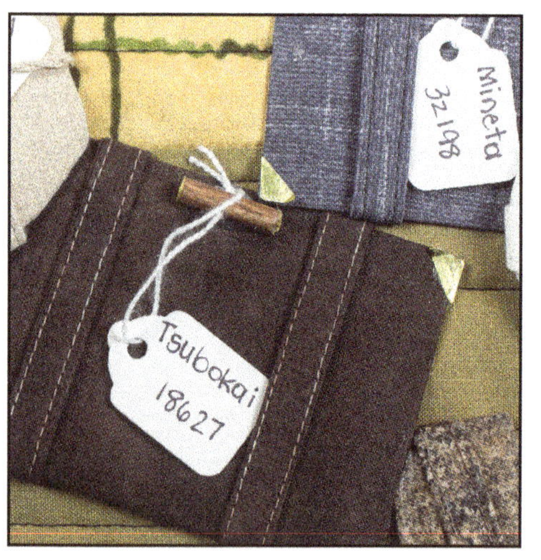

Jan Wilbur
Cody, Wyoming

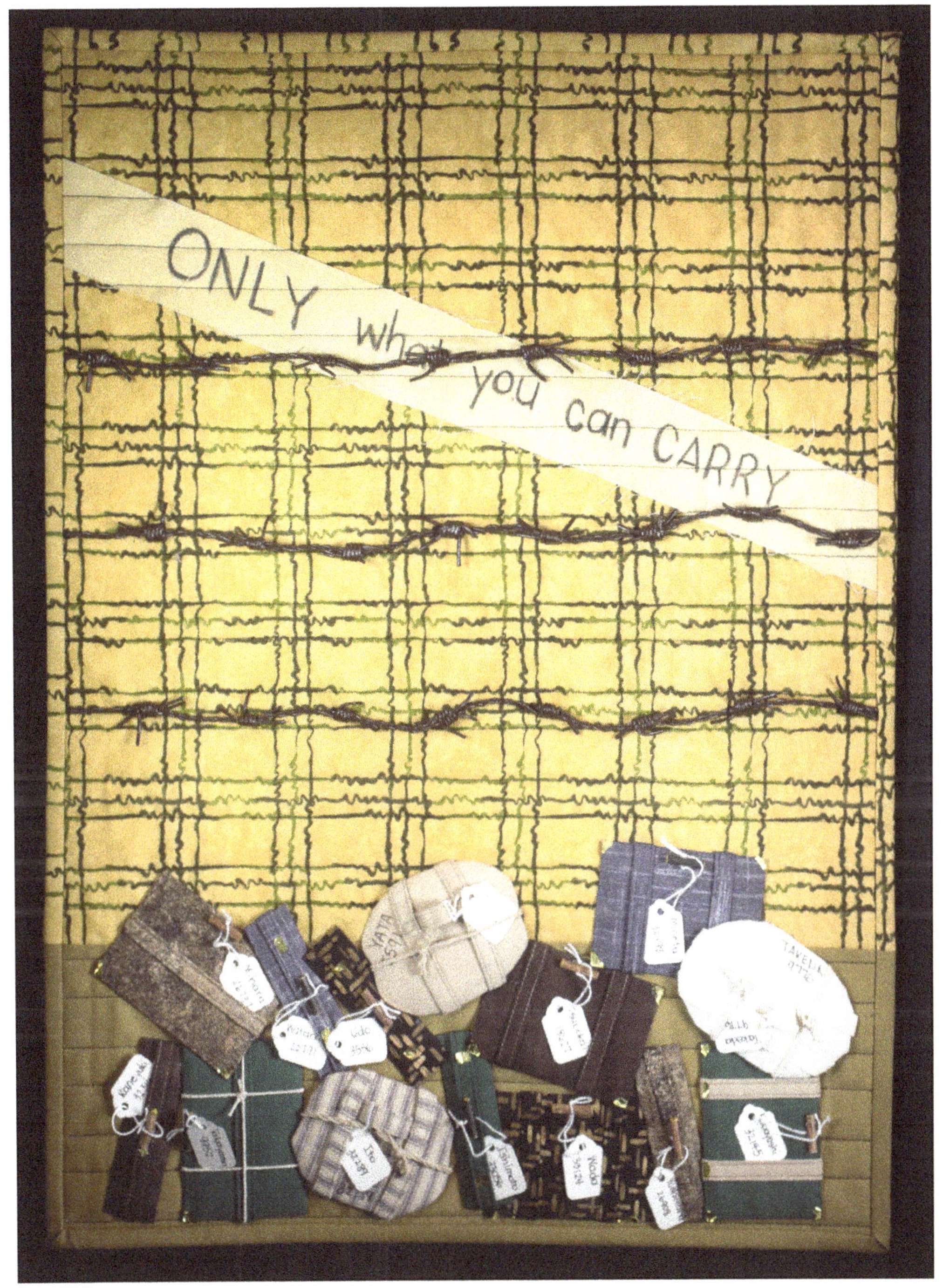

ONLY what you can CARRY

www.ingramcontent.com/pod-product-compliance
Lightning Source LLC
Chambersburg PA
CBHW042051030726
47599CB00019B/2452